The Civilization of the American Indian Series

REQUIEM FOR A PEOPLE

UNIVERSITY OF OKLAHOMA PRESS: NORMAN

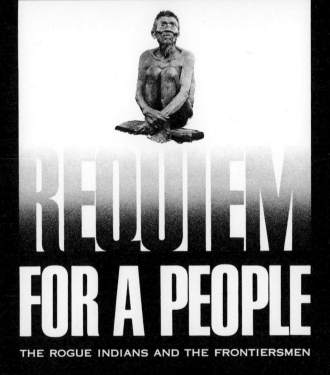

REQUIEM
FOR A PEOPLE

THE ROGUE INDIANS AND THE FRONTIERSMEN

Stephen Dow Beckham

International Standard Book Number: 0–8061–0942–4

Library of Congress Catalog Card Number: 79–145497

Copyright 1971 by the University of Oklahoma Press, Publishing Division of the University. Composed and printed at Norman, Oklahoma, U.S.A., by the University of Oklahoma Press. First edition.

Requiem for a People is Volume 108 in *The Civilization of the American Indian Series.*

To my parents,
Dow and Anna Beckham

PREFACE

SEVERAL YEARS AGO, perhaps in 1952 or 1953, I stood in the warm sun at a tumble-down post office called Illahe, Oregon. Seated there in a chair, looking as old as his ninety years revealed him to be, was George W. Meservey (1862–1963), the son of a Chetco Indian woman and Elisha Meservey, a miner, pioneer, adventurer, and volunteer in the Rogue wars nearly one hundred years before. Old Mr. Meservey, speaking slowly yet distinctly, recalled the stories of the former days, days that were as fresh to him as the swirling water in the nearby Rogue River. As I stood there, listening, absorbing, and looking up at the timbered hills above the Big Bend of the Rogue, I determined to find some day the full history of that land and its long-vanished people. The story was found, and it had to be written.

This task was made possible by many willing hands and fine friends. My sincere thanks to John W. and LaRee Caughey for their counsel, suggestions, and guidance at each stage of this work. Professor Caughey's criticisms and those of my fellow students in his seminars on Western history have assisted immeasurably. I also thank Professors Merlin Stonehouse and James Goss for reading the manuscript.

The libraries of the University of California, Los Angeles and Berkeley, and in particular the staff of the Bancroft Library in Berkeley, have extended their materials willingly and helpfully. I would like to thank Martin Schmitt and Elizabeth Findley of the University of Oregon Library and the staff members of the Oregon Historical Society Library in Portland, the California Historical Society Library in San Francisco, and the Coos-Curry Historical Museum in North Bend. Yale University Library has kindly allowed the reproduction of materials from their Western Americana collection.

The cartographic and war records divisions of the National Archives have willingly searched their files, answered questions, and provided valuable information. My appreciation is extended to Margaret C. Blaker of the Smithsonian Institution for the assistance of that archive.

Mention also needs to be made of the pleasant working atmosphere and the patient help given by the Hudson's Bay Company Archives of Great Trinity Lane, London, England. The staffs of the manuscript and ethnological divisions of the British Museum and the Public Record Office in London have likewise assisted with this work.

I would like to acknowledge aid from the American Indian History Study established at the University of California at Los Angeles by Doris Duke. Her grant provided generous assistance during the final preparation of this manuscript.

A number of individuals have answered questions and provided me with unpublished diaries, reminiscent accounts, and letters. I thank Gwenedde Maple, Alice Wooldridge, Fred B. Rogers, Wallace Wade, Robert Knox, John Adams, Frank Colvin, Ila Smith, Richard Fisk, Elizabeth Brunette, Edna Going, Lois Giles, Joe Harry, Mary Young Seibel, and Dorothy Bourns.

My brothers, David and Mark, I thank for their patience and enthusiasm during our many camping and hiking expeditions in the Rogue country.

And to my wife Patti, for her cheerful encouragement, I am ever grateful.

STEPHEN DOW BECKHAM

McMinnville, Oregon
January 23, 1971

CONTENTS

xi

ILLUSTRATIONS

xiii

THE ROGUE INDIANS AND THE FRONTIERSMEN

THE LAND AND THE PEOPLE

WITHIN THE SOUND of the constant roar of the Pacific's surf
on the southwestern Oregon coast is a dense thicket of spruce.
The sharp needles of the trees fold from limb to limb through
the moist air to filter out the sunlight which attempts to pene-
trate the solitude and rain-forest grandeur of the place. The
needles falling from these trees for centuries have carpeted
the ground. In a scarcely visible clearing, but one large
enough to allow a few pale huckleberry bushes to grow
gnarled and gaunt in the shadows, lies flat among the needles
a lichen-covered granite marker, lettered in an antique script.
It reads:

Sacred to the Memory of
JOHN GEISEL
Also his three Sons
John Henry
& Andrew
who were
Massacred by the Indians
Feb. 22, A.D. 1856.

A single fern frond, seldom stirred by the wind, reaches
across the top of this marker. The entire scene appears frozen
and unreal, but there in the forest deepness is a lingering
memory of an era when Indian and pioneer faced each other.
This was an era whose story has been told in almost endless
fashion as America was settled and the inhabitants of her

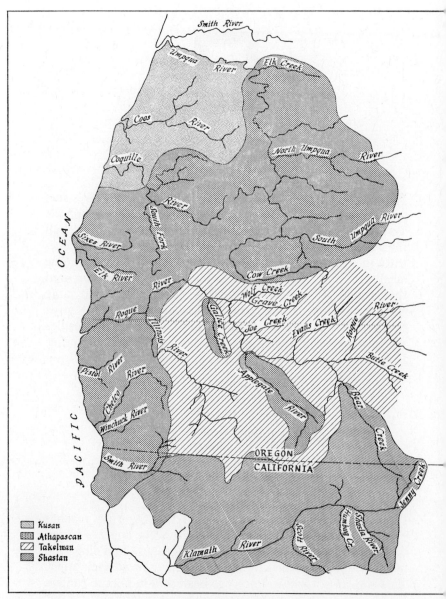

*Linguistic Distribution—Southwest Oregon and
Northern California*

forests, river valleys, and shores were forced to yield before the strong push of civilization.

This thicket is in the Rogue country, a corner of southwestern Oregon rugged in terrain and wet in climate. The Indians who once lived there were collectively referred to as the Rogues. These people, known for their fierce and roguish behavior, lived in a land well suited to their character.

Surrounded by mountains, the Rogue River flows between the ranges, and eventually through them, in a westerly course to the Pacific. It rises in the snow-covered Cascades. These largest and most spectacular mountains of the Rogue country are no longer fiery and volcanic. In once-explosive Mount Mazama rests the placid blue water of Crater Lake. The tallest peak in this section of the Cascades is a pinnacle cone, Mount McLoughlin, which holds its snowcap until the warming winds and long August days melt away the whiteness and leave scattered glaciers on its slopes above the timber line. With its base sometimes hidden in layers of clouds, this mountain looks down on the valley of the Rogue River.

Along the southern side of the valley are the ancient Siskiyous. These mountains are eroded and tree covered. On their slopes are serpentine outcroppings and boulders, freeze-shattered into gravel. Traces of nickel and tailings from mine shafts scatter down among the azaleas and rhododendrons growing on the hills. In the upper part of the valley the Siskiyous are drained by Bear Creek. Down river the Applegate River and Galice Creek empty into the Rogue. Farther west the Illinois River drains the limestone hills near the Oregon Caves and the swampy bottom lands in the prairies of the Josephine Valley. The Illinois wanders among the Siskiyous until it enters the Rogue about forty miles from the coast.

The northern edge of the Rogue Valley is formed by a series of tumbled hills referred to as the Umpqua Mountains. Although not high and seldom covered with snow, the Umpqua range was rugged enough to make the pioneers dread its slopes and canyons. These hills send Jump Off Joe Creek, Grave

Creek, and Wolf Creek into the Rogue. Cow Creek wanders through them, then suddenly swings away and flows into the South Umpqua.

Completing the four-walled chamber around the Rogue Valley is the Coast Range. Through these halfhearted mountains, which become indistinguishable from the Siskiyous, the Rogue River cuts a seventy-mile canyon from its valley to the ocean. At times the river is forced into narrow, deep channels, but occasionally it smooths into a still water which, when slightly brushed by the unfailing wind through these hills, shows no current.

The Rogue enters the Pacific along an almost harborless shore. The rivers which empty into the ocean in southern Oregon often throw a gravel bar across their mouths in the summer and seep into the ocean from stagnating lagoons. There are sections of sandy beaches, but rocky cliffs and sandstone hillsides, usually covered with a dense growth of windswept spruce and pine, follow close to the water. Early explorers along this coast named the headlands—Cape Ferrelo, Cape Sebastian, Cape Orford, and Cape Blanco.

The rains in the region, sometimes torrential, average about sixty-five inches a year. Along the coast are fogs spawned by the warm Japanese Current. They float toward the shore in the later afternoon and, though often leaving in the mornings, make some days entirely overcast and dismally gray. The sun seldom warms the coast to more than seventy-five degrees, but the mountains and valley of the Rogue often have a succession of days in the nineties. Night fogs and heavy dews linger in the ravines and dampen the green hills and fields in the Rogue Valley and the meadows along the Illinois. There are winter and early spring snows, but these quickly melt except in the higher elevations. The climate of the region is characterized as temperate.

Before the trader or explorer penetrated this region, and for yet a few years after the miner overturned the gravel bars with his shovel, pan, and sluice, and the settler plowed

6

under the camas lilies in the open river bottoms, three distinguishable linguistic groups of Indians shared this country.

The largest group among the Rogues was that speaking Athapascan dialects of the Na-Denean stock. This language family, the most widely distributed in North America, extended from Indians on the Yukon and Mackenzie rivers to the Apaches and the Navahos of the American Southwest. Two Athapascan tribes lived near the mouth of the Columbia River, but the largest representation of the Pacific branch of the linguistic family was located in southwestern Oregon and northern California.[1]

The Athapascans as well as other inhabitants of the Rogue country lived in villages that were nearly autonomous family units. Thus the term "tribe," where it signifies a political unity of people, cannot be applied to the Rogues.[2] However, a similarity of dialects and territorial proximity allows the following distinctions among the Athapascan speakers:[3]

Name of Band	Home Territory
Galice Creek and Applegate River	Tributary streams of Rogue below Rogue Valley.
Shasta Costa	Junctions of Illinois and Rogue upstream nearly to Rogue Valley.
Upper Coquille	Watershed of all forks of Coquille River.
Upper Umpqua	Watershed of Umpqua River except Elk and Calapuya creeks.
Tolowa	Lake Earl and Smith River (California) and Oregon's south coast.
Chetco	Chetco and Winchuck rivers.
Tututni	South of Coquille to Pistol River and up the Rogue to its junction with the Illinois.

[1] Joel V. Berreman, "Tribal Distribution in Oregon," *Memoirs, American Anthropological Association*, No. 47 (1937), 29.

[2] *Ibid.*, 31–32. Possible exceptions to this statement are indicated in the 1853 and 1854 reports that the Tututni were once a tribe of thirteen bands under Chal-Nah, a great headman. *California Farmer*, March 22, 1861. "Tututni" (MS).

[3] Berreman, "Tribal Distribution in Oregon," *loc. cit.*, 29–33.

The term "Tututni" was actually the name of people living in several villages a few miles upstream from the mouth of the Rogue River, but the early settlers in the region gave the word an extended meaning. As time passed, "Tututni" referred to all the scattered villages from as far north as the Coquille River to the isolated groups living along the shore south of Pistol River.

The Tututni, the Upper Umpqua, the Upper Coquille, and the Galice Creek people spoke dialects which were almost unintelligible to members of other bands.[4] Two Athapascan groups, those situated along the Applegate River and in its watershed in the Siskiyous and the bands on Galice Creek, were linguistic islands in the upper Rogue River country, surrounded by another language family. The two bands retained most of the distinctive Athapascan linguistic characteristics. Most familiar of these traits was the suffixing of "tunne," meaning "people," to a descriptive village name. Thus villages down river known as the Mikonotunne were the "people among the white clover roots"; the Tututni or Tututunne were the "people close to the river."[5]

In the Rogue Valley were the Dagelmas, "those living along the river," and the Latgawas, "those living in the uplands." Their linguistic family, Takelman, a Penutian stock limited entirely to western Oregon, was split into these two dialect groups. The Upland Takelmas lived above a volcanic shelf called Table Rock, which stands near the lower end of the valley. Below them on the Rogue, on upper Cow Creek, and in the Josephine Valley were the Lowland Takelmas.[6]

The third linguistic family of the Rogues was Shastan of the Hokan-Siouan stock. The Shastas, a tribe whose homeland was along a midsection of the Klamath River in north-

---

[4] *Ibid.*, 29.

[5] J. Owen Dorsey, "The Gentile System of the Siletz Tribes," *Journal of American Folklore*, Vol. III (1890), 233.

[6] Edward Sapir, "Notes on the Takelma Indians of South-western Oregon," *American Anthropologist*, New Series, Vol. IX (1907), 252. Berreman, "Tribal Distribution in Oregon," *loc. cit.*, 26–27.

ern California, were the Shastan speakers in Oregon. Some bands of these people, called the Scotans and the Shastas, spilled over the Siskiyous into the Rogue Valley. The lands they held were small. Some reports limit their territory to the drainage of Jenny Creek.[7] However, a treaty signed on November 18, 1854, by two bands of Shastas and three bands of Scotans relinquished claims to the watershed of Bear Creek, a tributary of the Rogue.[8]

No census was compiled while all the bands of the Rogues lived in their original homes. Occasional visitors to the region and Indian agents made partial surveys, but an accurate estimate of the total number of people is very difficult. However, in 1939, Alfred Kroeber, using a reworking of population figures compiled by James Mooney, set 8,800 as a probable number for the Athapascans and 500 for the Takelmas.[9] These figures were calculated to represent the population at the time of first white settlement, in this case 1851. No estimate was given for the Oregon Shastas, but at the time of their treaty in 1854 there were probably not more than about 250.[10]

Thus the Rogue country had an Indian population of about ninety-five hundred when the whites first began to settle. North of the Rogues on the coast were the Coos, another unique linguistic group numbering about two thousand.[11] North of the Upper Umpquas were the Umpquas, the Kalapuyas, and the Molallas. The Klamath and Modoc tribes lived east of the Cascades, while south of the Siskiyous

[7] Berreman, "Tribal Distribution in Oregon," *loc. cit.*, 27–28.

[8] Charles J. Kappler (ed.), *Indian Affairs: Laws and Treaties*, II, 655. Catherine Holt, "Shasta Ethnography," *University of California Anthropological Records*, Vol. III (1946), 301.

[9] "Cultural and Natural Areas of Native North America," *University of California Publications in American Archaeology and Ethnology*, Vol. XXXVIII (1939), 136.

[10] *Annual Report of the Commissioner of Indian Affairs, 1854*, 292–97.

[11] Kroeber, "Cultural and Natural Areas of Native North America," *loc. cit.*, 136.

9

dwelled the Shastas and the people of the lower Klamath River.

The cultural position of the Rogues was somewhat enigmatic. In many ways they were northern Californian, but they also possessed characteristics of the Northwest Coast culture and still other features which were clearly an adaptation to their own environment. Luther Cressman, writing about Takelman burials, stressed that the Rogue country was actually in a state to which it culturally did not belong.[12] Kroeber, similarly viewing the Rogues, classed them in the Lower Klamath Culture Area; that is, he allied them most closely with the tribes living along the lower Klamath River in northern California.[13]

The Lower Klamath Culture Area, which also included the Coos, contained an estimated nineteen thousand Indians in the early 1850's.[14] Kroeber placed this group as the southernmost extension of the Northwest Coast culture. However, these people did not use a wealth-destruction potlatch ceremony, totemic or clan system, large multifamily dwellings, or canoe burials, nor did they practice head-flattening.[15] They rarely held slaves, and in most cases the Rogues were the people sold into slavery by raiding parties of Shastas, Modocs, Klamaths, and Upland Takelmas.[16] The cultural intensity of the Rogues, as reflected in village size or artistic works, was measurably lower than that of the Chinooks, Salishes, and Nootkas. In spite of the varieties and modifica-

[12] "Aboriginal Burials in Southwestern Oregon," *American Anthropologist*, Vol. XXXV (1933), 124.

[13] "Types of Indian Culture in California," *University of California Publications in American Archaeology and Ethnology*, Vol. II, No. 3 (1904), 86.

[14] Kroeber, "Cultural and Natural Areas of Native North America," *loc. cit.*, 30.

[15] A. B. Lewis, "Tribes of the Columbia Valley and the Coast of Washington and Oregon," *Memoirs, American Anthropological Association,* Vol. I, Pt. 2 (1906), 147–209.

[16] H. G. Barnett, "Culture Element Distributions. VII. Oregon Coast," *University of California Anthropological Records*, Vol. I, No. 3 (1937), 185.

tions of life patterns in the Rogue country, the technology, myths, and physical appearance of the people were fairly uniform.[17]

The Rogues, largely forced by the land in which they lived, fractionalized into bands of from 30 to about 150 individuals. The favorite sites for their houses were the sandy bottom-land meadows along the rivers or near the creek mouths on the coast. When suitable windfalls or drift were not found, the men felled cedar trees with stone axes and used bone wedges and stone hammers to split the pliable, long-fibered lumber into planks.[18] They placed the slabs on end in the loamy soil around a pit three or four feet deep. Additional planks, resting on center supports, were overlapped for the roof. The entrance to the house was through a small elliptical hole in one end, and a notched log served as the ladder reaching to the floor. The dark interior was often filled with strings of dried venison, piles of smoked salmon, and a bountiful litter of broken shells, baskets, skins, and household implements.[19]

The Takelmas, who lived mostly east of the cedar forests, worked with the less pliable sugar pine. For that reason their houses often possessed only a brush roof and were sometimes more subterranean than the dwellings of their neighbors down river.[20]

These permanent houses were kitchens, pantries, and bedrooms for the Rogues. Ida Pfeiffer, an inquisitive round-the-world traveler, recorded her impressions of the housekeeping in some of the Chetco and Smith River villages on the coast in 1853:

It began to rain again, and the cold was so excessive that I

[17] Kroeber, "Cultural and Natural Areas of Native North America," *loc. cit.*, 30.

[18] Paul Schumacher, "Researches in the Kjökkenmöddings and Graves of a Former Population of the Coast of Oregon," *United States Geological and Geographical Survey of the Territories, Bulletin III*, No. 1 (1877), 29–30.

[19] *California Farmer*, March 22, 1861.

[20] Sapir, "Notes on the Takelma Indians," *loc. cit.*, 262–63.

11

was glad to find a place in one of these earth-holes, in the midst of the disgusting naked natives. We lay down round the fire, and about which half a dozen Indians were already crouching; but the hut soon became filled to overflowing with curious visitors, and the heat and vapors so suffocating that I was driven out again in despair, thinking I should prefer the rain and the cold.

Eventually the men left the house and Ida bedded down for the night with the women:

> One of them placed herself so close on one side of me, that I could hardly turn round; and on the other side, close to me, stood a large basket containing smoked fish; overhead hung another basket of fish to be smoked; and we lay on the bare cold ground, without a pillow or covering, so it may be imagined what a luxurious night I passed.[21]

This visitor's rest might have been even more fitful had she known that she was probably sleeping only a few feet above the ancestors of the women with whom she spent the night. The Rogues customarily buried their dead within the village, and, as years passed, new houses were frequently constructed over former cemeteries.[22]

From childhood the men slept in subterranean sweathouses located near the other dwellings in the villages. These low structures, lacking a plank floor that was sometimes used in the regular house, were dug into the ground, roofed over, and covered with earth so that they were nearly airtight. The occupants of the sweathouses often lay on tule mats and occasionally employed smooth willow poles as pillows.[23]

In addition to its service as a dormitory and fraternal retreat, the sweathouse was used in ceremonies and for curing disease. Dr. Rodney Glisan, a surgeon in the mid–1850's at

---

[21] *A Lady's Second Journey Round the World*, 314–15.

[22] Schumacher, "Researchers in the Kjökkenmöddings and Graves," *loc. cit.*, 32.

[23] Philip Drucker, "The Tolowa and Their Southwest Oregon Kin," *University of California Publications in American Archaeology and Ethnology,* Vol. XXXVI (1936), 272.

Fort Orford, about twenty miles north of the mouth of the Rogue River, noted that many of the fatalities among the Indians were not so much from consumption, smallpox, or measles as from the treatments. The afflicted people huddled in the smoky, dark sweathouses stoking the small fires that were steadily sapping them of their energy. Finally, when dripping with perspiration, they rushed out and plunged into the river or the ocean.[24]

Dr. Lorenzo Hubbard visited the coastal Rogues in 1853 and wrote that some of their ceremonies centered on the sweathouse. He described the zeal of the young men who attempted to endure near suffocation while sweating to prove their prowess. Many of the preparations for hunting expeditions were initiated with ritual purification in these Indian steam rooms.[25]

Ceremonies were of rather minor importance for the Rogues, though all the bands observed a "good time" dance and a war dance.[26] The Tututni practiced dances of warrior's purification, wealth display, and "doctor-fixing." The last was a five-night-long culmination to a novice shaman's fasting, bathing, and vigils. Chants from spectators and a "talker" or reciter kept the rhythm, for these people did not have drums.[27] When Oregon's Indian superintendent visited the Rogues at the mouth of the river in August, 1855, he witnessed this scene:

The spectators being seated on the ground, leaving an elliptical space in the middle for the dancers, some seventy or eighty persons will enter, and singing a he-ah ... ah, he-ah ... ah ... ah ... ah, will commence a succession of bobbing up and down, both feet at a time, body slightly bent, and limbs as rigid as marble statues. They all

[24] *A Journal of Army Life*, 253.

[25] *California Farmer*, March 22, 1861.

[26] Barnett, "Culture Element Distributions," *loc. cit.*, 192. Edward Sapir, "Religious Ideas of the Takelma Indians of Southwestern Oregon," *Journal of American Folklore*, Vol. XX, No. 76 (1907), 34–35.

[27] Barnett, "Culture Element Distributions," *loc. cit.*, 192.

spring in unison—and keep pretty good time. The same dance is kept up the whole night, with proper intervals of rest.[28]

The Rogues entertained themselves and taught their children about life, death, the gods, and nature by reciting myths. These Indians centered many of their stories on Coyote the trickster, the cleverest of all warriors—the being who could assume any physical appearance. The popularity of the mythical hero Coyote was a culture pattern followed by the tribes living in the Columbia River valley far to the north. The Rogues' tales about Loon-Woman and the Tar-Baby were similar to the myths of the tribes of northern California.[29]

One legend of the Rogues, a story recited years ago by Indian Mary, a woman of the Coquille band, portrays their joys, their sorrows, and their explanations of things unknown. Indian Mary told a story about the origin of the rock islands at the mouth of the Coquille River:

Seatco, evil spirit of the ocean, caused the storms that blew up and down the coast. He killed fish and threw them on the beach. Sometimes he swallowed canoes and fishermen. The coast people feared him and tried not to anger him.

The mountain tribes did not know Seatco, and so did not fear him. Whenever they came down to the coast to trade or to attend potlatches, they brought with them their families, horses, and dogs; the children brought their pets.

One summer, four chiefs of the coast Indians held a big potlatch in honor of Siskiyou, powerful chief of a mountain tribe. The four tribes planned a big feast, for they wanted to show their guests how prosperous the coast tribes were. The potlatch would be held on the beach, near the mouth of the Coquille River.

For days, the people were busy preparing the feast. The women and girls dug great numbers of clams and mussels and prepared them for steaming beneath sea moss and myrtle leaves. Hunters brought in a dozen elk and several deer. Many salmon were made

---

[28] Glisan, *A Journal of Army Life*, 252.

[29] Kroeber, "Types of Indian Culture in California," *loc. cit.*, 87–88. Leo J. Frachtenberg, "Shasta and Athapascan Myths from Oregon," *Journal of American Folklore*, Vol. XXVIII (1915), 207, 216.

ready for roasting on spits over driftwood fires. Huckleberries were heaped on cedar-bark trays. When runners announced that Chief Siskiyou and his people were a day's journey away, the roasting and the steaming were begun.

The chief brought with him his beautiful young daughter, and they camped on the potlatch grounds. The daughter, Ewauna, had her pets with her—her dog and a basket of baby raccoons. The girl had never before seen the ocean. All day long, she and her dog, Komax, raced along the beach, excited by the breaking of the waves.

People of the village warned her, "Don't go alone on the bluff. Seatco might see you and take you."

But Ewauna laughed at their warning.

By the morning of the second day all the guests had arrived, and the great feast began. The four chiefs, dressed in their ceremonial robes, welcomed their guests and spoke in praise of the great Chief Siskiyou. All day the hosts and guests feasted. That night they slept where they had eaten.

When all was quiet in the camp, the great chief's daughter, taking her dog and her basket of raccoons with her, slipped away to the beach. She ran and danced along the shore, singing a song to the moon, which hung low over the ocean. She danced nearer and nearer the water, into the silver path. Then she dropped her basket on the beach, told her dog to guard her little pets, and ran into the surf.

She would swim toward the moon, following the silver trail. Her dog barked a warning, but she swam on and on, far from shore. Suddenly a black hand passed across the moon, and she was seized by a creature that came out of the water. Seatco claimed her as his own and started toward his cliff with her.

The dog rushed to rescue her, carrying the basket of raccoons with him. He dropped the basket and sank his teeth into the demon's hand. Roaring with pain and anger, Seatco grabbed the dog and the basket and hurled them down the beach. He held the girl close to him, trying to make her look into his eyes. But she turned her face away and looked at the moon. She remembered that Seatco's power lay in his eyes.

Next morning the chief missed his daughter. He and his hosts rushed to the beach. The tide was out. The girl was lying on the wet

15

sand, her beautiful face looking up at the sky. Near by, her dog stood as if barking. A little west of them were the scattered raccoons and the empty basket. All had been turned to stone.

On a large rock near the shore sits Seatco, still trying to catch the eye of the maiden. He too has been changed to stone.[30]

Many of the superstitions and taboos of these people were associated with their food. The salmon, the staple throughout the year, they always split up the backbone with a stone knife. A youth's first salmon was taboo to his immediate family. These Indians burned over the hills near the entrance to the Rogue River, believing that this would induce the fish to enter the stream.[31]

The Rogues set up temporary camps along the beaches where the smelt spawn during the summer months. With scoop nets made of woven iris fibers and pounded roots, they gathered thousands of fish which perfumed the air while drying in the sun.[32] Indian women, searching the rocky shore, filled their burden baskets with mussels, clams, barnacles, and chitons. Occasionally the spearing of a seal or the stranding of a whale further enriched the diet.

Each band of the Rogues had favorite fishing rocks in the rivers. To these customary places, sometimes shared by several villages, the men brought their families and fishing equipment. Their lift nets, vine maple frames covered with woven mesh, easily captured a silvery flood of chinook or steelhead. When the run of fish was slight, the men fished the deeper pools with bone and horn hooks. Often nearly the whole population of a village manned the weirs in the rivers or their tributary streams. Men, women, and children, yelling and thrashing in the water, clubbed and speared the fish that would

[30] Ella E. Clark, *Indian Legends of the Pacific Northwest*, 124–26.

[31] Glisan, *A Journal of Army Life*, 248. Drucker, "The Tolowa and Their Southwest Oregon Kin," *loc. cit.*, 276–77. *California Farmer*, March 22, 1861.

[32] Alfred L. Kroeber, "Fishing among the Indians of North-Western California," *University of California Anthropological Records*, Vol. XXI (1960, 44–46, 179–80).

16

guarantee them a full stomach for another year. Their labor was wearisome, but the times of the salmon run were filled with fun, conversation, and, no doubt, romance.[33]

Another food-gathering activity, the digging of camas lily bulbs, also caused these people to leave their winter village sites. For the Takelmas and the Athapascans away from the coast these migrations to open prairies among the tanbark oaks, or to the rapids and fishing rocks along the river canyon, were necessary to insure an adequate food supply. The coastal bands had an abundance of fish, crabs, and shellfish, but villages like those of the Upland Takelmas in the foothills of the Cascades were forced to utilize nearly every edible food in order to survive. They ate grasshoppers, caterpillars, yellow jacket larvae, and snails in addition to their usual food of grass seeds, pine nuts, and acorns, and deer, fish, and elk meat.[34]

Second in importance to the salmon was the acorn. The women and children gathered the nuts as soon as they formed in the spring. After a ceremonial observance by the men, the women pounded the dried acorns into a crude flour with stone pestles. Their favorite working places were at deeply worn mortars carved into the bedrock overlooking the rivers. When the acorns were crushed, they poured hot water over the mash to leach out the bitter taste and the tannic acid. They thickened the flour into a mush by boiling it in baskets of tightly woven hazel shoots. The gruel was either eaten at once or baked near the coals of the fire as "sand bread."[35]

The varied skills and fine techniques of the Rogue women were readily employed for basketmaking. In anticipation of a new project they gathered hazel shoots, spruce roots, grasses, and ferns. When all was ready they patiently wove the hazel into the basic shape desired and decorated this foundation in

[33] Drucker, "The Tolowa and Their Southwest Oregon Kin," *loc. cit.*, 271.

[34] *Ibid.*, 294.

[35] Sapir, "Notes on the Takelma Indians," *loc. cit.*, 258.

17

intricate overweave of geometrical designs with bull grass and the stipe of the maidenhair fern.[36] Their nimble fingers constructed cradleboards for their infants, large storage baskets for acorns and dried salmon, and tightly woven containers to use in stone-boiling food. Good weavers produced baskets that were nearly watertight; a coat of hot pitch completed the task. By tossing in heated rocks, the Indian women brewed fish heads and tails, clams, crayfish, mussels, and a fair share of ashes and dirt.[37]

The Rogues used canoes for travel on the rivers and along the coast. These craft were built from single logs split by wedges. The men hollowed out the shell of the dugout with stone adzes and by burning, and softened the hull for the placement of thwarts by filling it with water and tossing in hot stones. They rubbed the outside of the canoe with oil, sometimes burning it over, and polished the surface with the scouring rush. They used paddles, occasionally with notched blades, for pushing off snags in swift water, and also spruce and fir poles to propel the canoes.[38]

In the spring of 1792, when vessels of Vancouver's exploring expedition anchored near the foamy and rock-scattered surf at Cape Blanco, Archibald Menzies, a surgeon and botanist aboard the *Chatham*, recorded a visit from some of the Rogues who lived along the shore:

Their Canoe was by no means calculated to go far to sea or enduring much bad weather, it had some distant resemblance to a Butchers Tray being truncated at both ends short broad and shallow. It was about 18 feet long 4 feet & ½ broad, in the middle but a little narrower toward the ends, & it was about 2 feet deep formd of one piece of Pine Tree dug out & tolerably well finished.[39]

---

[36] Alfred L. Kroeber, "Basket Designs of the Indians of North-western California," *University of California Publications in American Archaeology and Ethnology*, Vol. II (1904), 109.

[37] Pfeiffer, *A Lady's Second Journey Round the World*, 315.

[38] Drucker, "The Tolowa and Their Southwest Oregon Kin," *loc. cit.*, 272.

[39] "A. Menzies Journal of Vancouver's Voyage, 1790–1794" (MS), 215–16.

Other narratives give similar descriptions of these dugouts which could hold as many as ten men. The canoes had blunt raised ends, inturned gunwales, and a carved steersman's seat. In addition to this type the Upper Coquilles also used a double-pointed dugout known to the Coos Indians.[40]

When the Tututni visited the Vancouver ships, they quickly tied alongside and boarded the vessels, showing their "mild & peaceable dispositions." Menzies wrote:

Most of them appeared on our Decks naked having left their garments which were made from squirrel racoon & deer skins in the Canoe; they wore caps on their heads made from the breast and belly parts of Shag skins which fitted them very close & comfortable; Each of them had his ears & the septum of his nose perforated, in the latter some of them wore an ornament made of the tooth shell but which they readily parted with on thrusting a small nail in the place of it. . . . They were of a middling size with mild pleasing features & nowise sullen or distrustfull in their behaviour, they were of a copper colour but cleanly, as we observed no vestige of greasy paint or ochre about their faces or among their hair, some had their bodies marked in various directions & some were Tatooed in different parts.[41]

The Takelma men wore shirts, buckskin leggins or trousers, moccasins, and sometimes blankets of deerskin. They made their hats of bear or deer scalps and often left the ears attached. The women of the Rogue Valley wore buckskin dresses, fringed with tassels of white grass, reaching to their knees. Their hats were of a round basket type of twined grass and were obtained from the Shastas by trade.[42] The men and women on the coast wore their hair in a long roll which they smoothed with their fingers and twisted around their heads with a piece of skin or ragged cloth. The tourist Ida Pfeiffer would have recommended additional grooming, for she noted:

[40] Drucker, "The Tolowa and Their Southwest Oregon Kin," *loc. cit.*, 272, 279–80.
[41] Menzies, "A. Menzies Journal," *loc. cit.*, 215–16.
[42] Sapir, "Notes on the Takelma Indians," *loc. cit.*, 263–64.

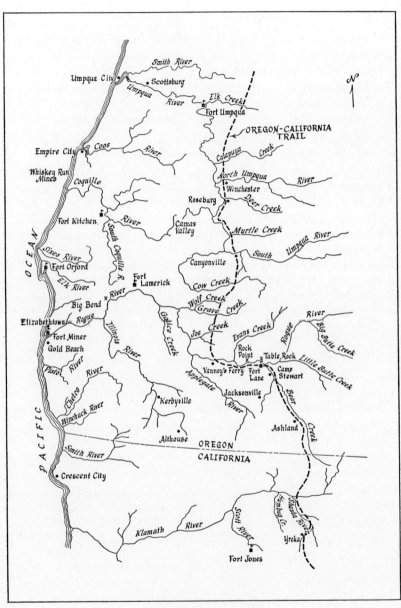

The Rogue Country

"I have seen them, for instance, searching in each other's heads for vermin, and presenting the specimens they found conscientiously to the owner, who actually devoured them!"[43]

Most colorful about the dress of the Rogues was their penchant for bright red scalps of the woodpecker. The Takelmas sewed this patch of feathers, with the beak usually still attached, on strings of buckskin and wore it in a band tied around their heads and dangling down their backs. To these strips they often attached treasured white dentalium shells which they acquired by trade from Puget Sound. The Takelma women fastened these strips to their scalp and allowed the feathers, shells, and their hair to hang down from underneath their basket-caps. The shamen were yet more elaborate. They used otter skins and feathers from the eagle and the yellow-hammer to enhance their clothing and sometimes added tassels of grass and porcupine quills.[44]

These woodpecker scalps, dentalium shells, and deer-skins, especially the rare hides of albino deer, were highly valued by the Rogues who, like the Northwest Coast people, put great emphasis on wealth. The ownership of a slab house, a dugout canoe, many strings of dentalia, or a fine collection of feathers contributed significantly to an individual's esteem and prestige among these people.[45]

Each Rogue village, commonly referred to as a "rancheria" by early settlers in the region, was an extended patrilineal family with marriage outside the local unit. Maternally related individuals could marry, but often the husband and wife came from bands speaking different dialects or even different languages. Marriage was usually decided by the parents of the couple at an early age. The girl was always obtained by purchase with dentalia shells by the father of the boy. Mutual exchange of baskets and other gifts then occur-

---

[43] *A Lady's Second Journey Round the World*, 317.
[44] Sapir, "Notes on the Takelma Indians," *loc. cit.*, 263–65.
[45] Cora DuBois, "The Wealth Concept as an Integrating Factor in Tolowa-Tututni Culture," in *Essays in Anthropology Presented to A. L. Kroeber*, 60–62.

red; however, the couple did not live together until they had reached maturity. The social standing of children was determined by the price which had been paid for their mother. A son-in-law was further obliged to give additional presents to his wife's parents. Wealthy men could possess several wives.[46]

The Rogues loved to play at the fishing weir, gamble about the outcome of their cricket-like shinny games, fight with their neighbors, and carve their marks on boulders along the river. They left unnoticed the gold that glittered in their streams. Beaver, otter, and other game were abundant, but they killed only to supply their needs. Except for the digging sticks of the women, they left the fertile meadows untouched. They were a Stone Age people in a ruggedly beautiful and rich land.

[46] Drucker, "The Tolowa and Their Southwest Oregon Kin," *loc. cit.*, 273. Sapir, "Notes on the Takelma Indians," *loc. cit.*, 274–75. Edward S. Curtis, *The Hupa, Yurok, Karok, Wiyot, Tolowa and Tututni, Shasta, Klamath*, 230.

THE OPENING OF THE ROGUE COUNTRY

THE FIRST APPROACHES of white men to the Rogue country were from the sea. Spanish interest in California brought sailing vessels nosing along the Pacific coast, spying out headlands, capes, islands, and occasionally river mouths. The discoveries and adventures of these voyagers are almost as shrouded as the cloudy coast they visited. In the late eighteenth century, however, the otter trade attracted dozens of enterprising vessels to the Northwest Coast. As early as 1788, during Captain Robert Gray's first journey to the Pacific on the *Columbia Revidia*, the crewmen noticed the populous Indian villages along the shore.

In April, 1792, three sailing ships scudded before the wind along the coast of the Rogue country. Gray, on his second epoch-making voyage, traded for skins with natives who paddled out to his vessel between the Umpqua and Coos Bay. His trade with the Indians was brisk and satisfying to both parties. The appearance of the Indians was fierce and no doubt influenced John Boit, one of Gray's shipmates, to write: "I'm fearfull these fellows are caniballs."[1] That same month, Captain George Vancouver's sloop of war, the *Discovery*, and its armed tender, the *Chatham*, met Indians off Cape Blanco.[2]

The coastal Indians of southwestern Oregon became accus-

[1] Frederick W. Howay (ed.)., *Voyages of the* Columbia *to the Northwest Coast, 1787–1790 and 1790–1793*, 30–31, 392.
[2] Peter Puget, "Log of Discovery, 1791–1792" (MS), 88.

tomed to the visits of the sailing ships. Although the rich supplies of otter were rapidly depleted, persistent traders continued to work the region for many years. No doubt their experiences were much like those of the crew of the British vessel *Columbia* which drew near the wind-swept headlands of Cape Blanco in July, 1817. The men found that the cape, covered with a stocky spruce forest, pushed far into the sea. From the small valleys of the Sixes and Elk rivers—streams entering the ocean to the north and south of the promontory— and from camps along the beach rose telltale columns of smoke.

These British traders found that the Indians no longer displayed the curiosity and the "mild & peaceable dispositions" that the Vancouver expedition had found twenty-five years before. To be sure, the Indians paddled out to the *Columbia* in their canoes, but they seemed extremely cautious. Peter Corney, a diarist aboard the vessel, wrote that the men were holding green boughs and bunches of feathers. After one of the Indians uttered a gutteral and incomprehensible speech, the men, singing lustily, paddled closer to the ship. "When they came alongside," Corney recorded, "we gave them a rope and made signs for them to come on board, which nothing could induce them to do; they seemed quite terrified."[3]

Experience had taught the Rogues prudence in their dealings with the white men. Evidence of the intercourse between the peoples of the coast and the trading ships, however, remains in the region. When the winter winds blow along the cliffs through the middens, scraps of metal, tarnished thimbles and buttons, dozens of blue and white beads, and, rarely, small bells cast in China appear on the surface. These visible remains speak for the increasing awareness the Indian had of the white man from across the sea.

Less than three years after the *Columbia* visited southern Oregon, a hardy fur trapper attempted to enter the region by land. Thomas McKay, one of the earliest explorers of the

3 *Voyages in the Northern Pacific,* 77–78.

Willamette Valley, battled the Indians living along the Umpqua River and withdrew.[4]

During the spring and summer of 1826, Alexander Roderick McLeod, accompanied by four white men and nine Indians, journeyed along the Oregon coast gathering furs. He returned to the Columbia River in August and reported that the Indians had told him of a river that abounded in beaver two days beyond his coastal camp.[5]

John McLoughlin, the ambitious new factor of the Hudson's Bay Company in the Pacific region, immediately decided to outfit a strong brigade and dispatched it to the rich land to the south. David Douglas, a British botanist collecting in the Northwest, joined these men. Douglas, while a guest at Fort Vancouver, had learned from an Indian that large pines grew along the upper reaches of the Umpqua River. His scientific curiosity was aglow, and, though the journey would mean hardships, the botanist readied his notebooks, press, and camping equipment.

When the brigade reached the Umpqua, Douglas left the trappers and traveled alone into the forested hills through which the river wandered before it turned to the sea. The Englishman was no woodsman. After a pleasant visit at an Indian village, Douglas attempted to build a raft to cross the river, but he blistered his hands so badly that he had to abandon the project. Later, while pursuing a large buck which he had wounded, Douglas tumbled into a ravine and lay stunned for several hours until some friendly Indians found him and helped him back to their village.[6]

Dispirited, Douglas returned to the trappers' base camp, but within a few days he was again eager to try another

[4] E. E. Rich (ed.), *The Letters of John McLoughlin from Fort Vancouver to the Governor and Committee. Second Series, 1839–1844*, 114.

[5] E. E. Rich (ed.), *The Letters of John McLoughlin From Fort Vancouver to the Governor and Committee. First Series, 1825–38*, 30.

[6] David Douglas, "Sketch of a Journey to the Northwestern Parts of the Continent of North America, During the Years 1824-'25-'26-'27," *Oregon Historical Quarterly*, Vol. VI, No. 1 (1905), 84–85.

search for the pines of southern Oregon. In late October he set out with an Indian guide. When his companion at last declined to travel farther, the botanist pushed alone up the South Umpqua River. On October 26 he met an Indian who instantly strung his bow. Douglas made a friendly gesture to this man by offering him his pipe; then he sketched the cones and the trees he was seeking. The Indian understood and pointed to the mountains to the south. The two headed for the area.

Douglas found his pines, but they were too large to fell and he was unable to discover cones on the ground. "I endeavored," he wrote, "to knock off the cones by firing at them with ball, when to the report of my gun brought eight Indians, all of them painted with red earth, armed with bows, arrows, bone-tipped spears and flint knives." For a few minutes the botanist faced the Indians, but when he made them understand that he would give them tobacco if they would find him some cones, the men disappeared. As soon as the Indians were gone, Douglas grabbed some twigs and other specimens and fled.[7]

This first explorer in the upper Umpqua area eventually worked his way down the river. Douglas spent several frightening nights in his rain-soaked tent while trees fell about him with thundering crashes. As winter arrived, Douglas finally stumbled into the camp of the Hudson's Bay Company men. He waited at this site near the ocean until Alexander McLeod arrived. McLeod had traveled south to Coos Bay and on to the Coquille River where he learned from the Indians about a still larger stream farther to the south. Not until January 11, 1827, did McLeod make the journey to the mouth of the Rogue River.[8]

Douglas and McLeod and the other land explorers of the brigade were well received by the Indians of the lower Ump-

---

[7] *Ibid.*

[8] Alice Bay Maloney, "Camp Sites of Jedediah Smith on the Oregon Coast," *Oregon Historical Quarterly*, Vol. XLI, No. 3 (1940), 310.

qua. "All the natives," noted Douglas, "like those in this neighborhood, had never seen white men before, and viewed them narrowly, and with great curiosity. They were kind and hospitable in the extreme, assisting to kindle the fire and make the encampment."[9]

The quest for beaver brought other adventurers into southern Oregon in 1827. Peter Skene Ogden, leader of the Hudson's Bay Company brigades that worked the Snake River country, reached Klamath Lake in December, 1826. In January and February, Ogden dispatched trappers to the streams draining Mount Shasta and also sent a party far down the Klamath River. During March, Ogden and his men crossed the Siskiyou Mountains and camped on the banks of the Rogue River. These explorers were the first to enter the heartland of the Rogue country. They learned that the Umpquas had already visited the region, gathering furs to trade to McLeod, who had visited their villages. Ogden, nevertheless, ordered four of his party to trap the beaver in the mountains north of the valley, and, if possible, find their way to Fort Vancouver. The men journeyed to the headwaters of the Umpqua, and, as they worked their way downstream, they recognized where they were. They reached McLoughlin's headquarters that spring. Ogden and the remainder of his party left the Rogue Valley on April 7, returning to Klamath Lake.[10]

In June, 1828, eighteen weary men approached the Rogue country from the south. Traveling through the brush and canyons along the Trinity and Klamath rivers, Jedediah Smith and his party eventually entered the redwood forests near the coast. Hunger had caused them to kill their last dog for food, and necessity had taught them to trade eagerly with the Indians for mussels, eels, and berries. Sickness and lack of

[9] Douglas, "Sketch of a Journey," *loc. cit.*, 95.
[10] T. C. Elliott (ed.), "The Peter Skene Ogden Journals," *Oregon Historical Quarterly*, Vol. XI, No. 2 (1910), 217. Rich (ed.), *Letters of John McLoughlin, First Series, 1825–38*, 44–45.

fodder for their three hundred pack animals compounded their difficulties.[11]

Clinging to coast Indian trails, the Smith expedition reached the south side of the Chetco River on June 24. Near their camp were ten or a dozen lodges, but the inhabitants of the village fled when they saw the white men. The night passed quietly, but the next day some of the horses were found trapped in the Indians' deadfall elk pits. Two pack animals were wounded with arrows, and one horse was missing. The party crossed the Chetco at low tide and followed the beach trail until the rock ravines and brush-covered hillsides north of Cape Ferrelo forced them onto the high ridges. On June 27 they reached the Rogue River. Smith was impressed by the large quantity of fresh water at the mouth of the river and correctly assumed that the stream was of good size.[12]

The party traveled five to twelve miles a day along the coast and on July 3 reached the Coquille. Since the stream appeared deep, Smith particularly desired to borrow some canoes to assist during the crossing. Four Indians, startled at seeing this large band of intruders coming to the riverbank, rushed to their canoe and paddled madly upstream. Smith wheeled his horse about and dashed along the shore to intercept them. To his dismay, the Indians drew their canoe upon the mud and at once split it to pieces with their stone hammers.[13]

Five days' travel brought the Smith party to Coos Bay, and, although the men were cordially received by the "Cahoose" Indians, eight horses and mules were shot with arrows. The pack animals waded across the wide sand bar at the mouth of the harbor while Smith and his men used borrowed canoes. The eighteen journeyed north on a windy, cold day through miles of sand dunes crowding the coast between the Umpqua and the Coos. When they reached the Umpqua,

---

[11] Maurice Sullivan (ed.), *The Travels of Jedediah Smith*, 92–95.
[12] *Ibid.*, 101–104
[13] *Ibid.*, 105.

the river so recently visited by Douglas and McLeod, the travelers camped about four miles upstream from the ocean. The Kalawatsets, the band inhabiting the lower river and coast, stormed this camp on July 14. The attack was a dreadful massacre; fourteen of the party were murdered. Four survivors, including Smith, ultimately reached Fort Vancouver nearly two hundred miles to the north.[14]

The massacre of the Smith party brought an immediate reaction from the Hudson's Bay Company, whose policy was to tolerate no Indian hostility. In October, McLeod, Smith, and others returned to the Umpqua to recover the furs, journals, and pack animals and to learn the fate of the thirteen men and the young helper who were missing. Near the mouth of the Umpqua on October 28, McLeod poignantly wrote in his journal:

Stopped at the entrance of the North Branch, where Mr. Smith's Party were destroyed and a Sad spectacle of Indian barbarity presented itself to our View, the Skeletons of eleven of those Miserabl Sufferers lying bleaching in the Sun . . . no Indians in the Vicinity, contrary to their former Custom as several Villages used to be about this place the Natives are now more collected than formerly.[15]

The McLeod-Smith expedition remained on the coast for the first two weeks of November. With diligent searching and rigorous questioning, the men were able to recover a few copper kettles, furs, diaries, and horses. Considering the matter closed, they did not attack the Kalawatsets.

This hostility of the Indians did not stop the Hudson's

14 Maloney, "Camp Sites of Jedediah Smith," loc. cit., 317–18, 320. Those killed were Thomas Virgin, Tousant Marreshall, Joseph Palmer, Joseph Lapoint, Morion (an Indian boy), Harrison G. Rogers, Martin McCoy, Peter Raney, John Gaiter, John Hannah, Abraham Laplant, Manuel Lazarus, Thomas Daw, and Charles Swift. Jedediah Smith, William Sublette, and David E. Jackson, "A Brief Sketch of accidents, misfortunes, and depredations committed by Indians, etc., on the firm of Smith, Jackson, and Sublette, since July 1826 to the present 24th, 1829" (MS).

15 Sullivan, (ed.), Travels of Jedediah Smith, 128–29.

Bay Company activity in southwest Oregon. During the next twenty years several different sites on the Umpqua became trading centers. Near the mouth of Calapuya Creek was Fort McKay; McLeod stayed there in October, 1828, and referred to the camp on the north side of the river as the "Site of the Old Establishment."[16] Fort Umpqua, opposite the mouth of Elk Creek and present Elkton, was established during the summer of 1836.[17] The chief trader and resident clerk at this latter post was Jean Baptiste Gagnier, a French-Canadian. Fort Umpqua, now a mound in an open meadow by the river, was the first permanent thrust of the white man into the region inhabited by the Athapascan speakers of southern Oregon. Although never a flourishing post, in 1847 it possessed five permanent buildings, a stockade twelve feet high and ninety feet square, and eighty acres of land under cultivation. The post was destroyed by fire on November 15, 1851.[18]

The trade in southwest Oregon was the usual assignment of Michel Laframboise, a pioneer in the fur business who had arrived on the Pacific Coast in 1811 aboard Astor's ill-fated *Tonquin*. Laframboise took his Umpqua brigade down the Oregon Coast in 1832, following a route first opened to San Francisco Bay by McLeod during the winter of 1828–29.[19] One of the trappers in Laframboise' party was John Turner, a survivor of the Umpqua massacre of 1828. This expedition of sixty-three men, women, and children and several Indians joined in California a brigade led by John Work. The Work party had reached the Sacramento by journeying through eastern Oregon and following rivers into the mountains to the west until it entered the great valley of Cali-

16 B 223/a/5 (MS).
17 B 223/b/15, fo. 33 (MS).
18 B 223/b/39, fo. 95d (MS). "Minutes of Council, Northern Department, 1832/50" (MS). Socrates Schofield, "The Klamath Exploring Expedition, 1850," *Oregon Historical Quarterly*, Vol. XVII, No. 4 (1916), 356. T. C. Elliott, "British Values in Oregon, 1847," *Oregon Historical Quarterly*, Vol. XXXII, No. 1 (1931), 41.
19 Rich (ed.), *Letters of John McLoughlin, First Series, 1825–38*, 111–12.

fornia. Neither Work or Laframboise felt that their trappers had found sufficient furs for an immediate return to Fort Vancouver; so joining forces, the brigades spent the spring of 1833 trading and trapping on the California coast between San Francisco and Cape Mendocino.[20]

By June, Laframboise was baling his furs and preparing to leave California. He led his men through the watershed of the Eel River, across the Trinity Alps, and north through the Rogue Valley to the Willamette. At almost the same time a second expedition entered the heart of the Rogue country. Turner, who had quit the Laframboise brigade in California, guided Ewing Young's men along the Oregon coast to the Umpqua River. After working upstream, the Young party swung south toward California, passing through the Rogue Valley to Klamath Lake.[21]

Work, too, eventually decided to return to Fort Vancouver. His party of twenty-eight men, twenty-two women, and forty-four children left the Sacramento Valley in midsummer. His expedition had been a very unrewarding one: the trappers took few furs, and the entire party experienced great misery and tribulation. The journey through the Rogue country was nearly the crushing blow to the expedition. Work guided his people in that direction after discovering Laframboise' trail north of Mount Shasta. On September 16, 1833, the fever-ridden party crossed the Siskiyous and camped on Bear Creek, a small fork of the Rogue River. That evening some peaceful Shasta Indians visited the travelers.[22]

On the seventeenth one of the trappers died, leaving a widow and six children. On the nineteenth the bleak, cold

[20] Alice Bay Maloney, "John Work of the Hudson's Bay Company: Leader of the California Brigade of 1832–33," *California Historical Society Quarterly*, Vol. XXII, No. 2 (1943), 102.

[21] *Ibid.*, 102–103. Alice Bay Maloney (ed.), "Fur Brigade to the Bonaventura: John Work's California Expedition of 1832–33 for the Hudson's Bay Company," *California Historical Society Quarterly*, Vol. XXII, No. 4 (1943), 330–31.

[22] Maloney (ed.), "Fur Brigade to the Bonaventura," *loc. cit.*, Vol. XXIII, No. 2 (1944), 139.

weather and poor grazing continued. Finally, on the twentieth the party reached the Rogue River, but the Indians fired volleys of arrows from the brush-covered hillsides and wounded several of the pack animals. As the people followed the trail into the mountains below the Rogue Valley, they discovered the campsites of the Laframboise and Young expeditions.[23]

The torrential rains made the crossing of each tributary of the Rogue a major undertaking. The fevers and sickness continued unabated. Some days the trappers did not even break camp. On the twenty-second the Indians gathered on the opposite side of the river from the camp, built a large fire, and greatly alarmed the party by screaming and yelling wildly. Work noted in his journal: "I was in a paroxysm of the fever and could not stir out. Owing to our helpless state, there being only 15 men in health in the camp, I felt uneasy for some time." The Indians left, but more days passed with little progress. Although the weather improved, the hunters could not find game. On September 26 another man died. "The people are getting more discouraged every day," concluded Work's entry.[24]

Finally, on October 3 the Work party left the Rogue's watershed. Ten days later they met Laframboise, who was out on another expedition. His party of sixty-three had reached Fort Vancouver the previous July. The survivors of the Work expedition, the second large overland party from California to Oregon, arrived at Fort Vancouver late in October, 1833.[25]

The Oregon–California land route was established. Perhaps as many as 250 had crossed over it and through the Rogue Valley in 1833. Slowly and sporadically, other parties also used this trail. In time the route became a familiar one, but nearly every passage was contested by the Indians who claimed this land.

During the summer of 1834 the adventurer Ewing Young

[23] *Ibid.*, 139–40.
[24] *Ibid.*, 140.
[25] *Ibid.*, 142–44.

and the aspiring empire-builder Hall J. Kelley enlisted four-teen men and gathered about one hundred horses and mules at Monterey and San Jose for an expedition to colonize Oregon. The party, probably entirely American, contained a number of ruffians. These men murdered several Indians while passing through the Sacramento Valley and also killed two young warriors who visited their camp on an island in Rogue River. The murderers said they feared the men would tell the Rogues about the weak condition of the party—Kelley and most of the others had malaria. The expedition had crossed the Umpqua Mountains before the Rogue River people discovered the bodies. The party arrived safely on the Willamette, but the murderous behavior of these Americans in southern Oregon was not forgotten by the Indians.[26]

Reportedly, other troubles occurred in the region the same year. John Turner, well known in the Willamette settle-ments for his adventures in southern Oregon, had joined four-teen settlers to go to California to purchase cattle. The Ore-gonians were attacked at the base of the Siskiyou Mountains, and the Indians, deadly in their ambush, massacred ten of the men. Turner killed four warriors and escaped with his surviving companions to the Willamette.[27]

The schemes and dreams of Young and Kelley encour-aged other Americans to come to Oregon. In the spring of 1835 seven men and their well-seasoned guide, John Turner, left Monterey to follow the trail from the Sacramento to the Columbia. The men disappeared, swallowed in the wilderness, and nothing was heard from them until August. On the twentieth a visitor at Fort Vancouver, the naturalist John K. Townsend, wrote in his journal: "Several days since a

26 Hall J. Kelley, *Hall Jackson Kelley on Oregon: A Collection of Five of His Published Works and a Number of Hitherto Unpublished Letters*, 252–53. S. A. Clarke, *Pioneer Days of Oregon History*, I, 296–97. A detailed narrative of this expedition appears in Chapter 7, "North to Oregon," in Kenneth L. Holmes, *Ewing Young: Master Trapper*.

27 George M. Colvocoresses, *Four Years in a Government Exploring Expedition*, 276–77.

poor man came here in a most deplorable condition, having been gashed, stabbed, and bruised in a manner truly frightful." The nearly delirious fellow had struggled afoot for fifteen days from the Rogue Valley.[28]

When his wounds were treated and he was fed, Dr. William Bailey told his hosts of the ambush that befell his party in southern Oregon. A few days later three more survivors arrived on the Columbia. One of them was Turner, the intrepid survivor of so many of the troubles with the Indians of the Rogue country. Four of the Americans were killed in this massacre.[29]

As Hudson's Bay Company employees retired and new settlers slowly took up lands along Oregon's fertile river bottoms, an increasing need for cattle developed in the region. Cattle at that time could be readily acquired only in California. When Ewing Young's attempts to establish a brewery in the Willamette Valley met the strong disapproval of both the Hudson's Bay Company and the Methodist Mission, he sailed on February 10, 1837, to California to search for another means of profit. Fighting contradictions and whims of Mexican officials, Young was finally able to purchase about 730 head of cattle. In September the fifteen tired, overworked men driving the herd neared the Siskiyous. Three of the drovers were Bailey, Turner, and Gay, survivors of the 1835 massacre.[30]

On September 14, along the Klamath River, Bailey and Gay shot an Indian boy who was standing near their camp. This provocative deed alarmed the other drovers, and all the men feared that the Indians might retaliate. The hardships and the ill will among the men exploded the next day in a wild quarrel. After fifteen minutes of fighting each other with fists, guns, and knives, the drovers realized the foolish-

---

[28] John K. Townsend, *Narrative of a Journey across the Rocky Mountains, to the Columbia River*, 328–29.
[29] Hubert Howe Bancroft, *History of Oregon: 1834–1848*, 95–96.
[30] *Ibid.*, 143, 147–50.

ness of their actions and the gravity of their situation, declared a truce, and returned to the arduous job of driving the cattle over the mountains.[31]

Near noon on September 18, at the favorite ambush site of the Rogues near Rocky Point in the narrow canyon below the valley, the Indians struck. The cattle were scattered along the trail, but the men managed to charge forward at the main body of the Indians. The Rogues wounded Gay and put two arrows in Young's horse. The cattle company met no further trouble; in October the drovers arrived in the Willamette Valley. One hundred head of cattle had perished during the journey, but 630 animals were safe in Oregon to greatly buttress the livestock of that region.[32]

Shortly after Young and the cattle arrived in Oregon, the missionary Jason Lee left the Methodist settlement in the Willamette Valley to investigate the Umpqua region. He went there to learn the number of Indians and the prospects for establishing a mission. The winter rains restricted his survey; he had to rely on questioning Indians and the resident trader at Fort Umpqua. Lee's interest in southwest Oregon was whetted. Returning to the East Coast the next year, he secured Rev. Gustavus Hines and an assistant as recruits to extend the ministry to the Umpqua.[33]

By August, 1840, Lee was back in Oregon prepared to continue his survey for a new mission. He arrived at Fort Umpqua on August 22 with Dr. Elijah White, Rev. Hines, and an Indian guide. Of the fort Hines wrote: "Not long since the place was attacked by a band of savages, outnumbering ten times the inmates of the fort, but after a long fight in which no one was killed, and but two or three of the Indians were wounded, the latter were compelled to retreat."[34]

[31] Philip L. Edwards, *The Diary of Philip Leget Edwards: The Great Cattle Drive from California to Oregon in 1837*, 43–44.

[32] *Ibid.*, 46–47.

[33] Gustavus Hines, *Wild Life in Oregon*, 94–95.

[34] *Ibid.*, 99.

After traveling by canoe to the coast and returning, Lee and Hines went up the river, probably following much the same route as the botanist Douglas. Their impressions of the prospects for a mission were not favorable, for the Umpquas were scattered, and the greatest number of villages were on the inaccessible coast. Lee preached and Hines sang hymns, but the people seemed to be beyond their Methodist ministry. Hines, rather prophetically, summed up their trip:

> Under the impression that the doom of extinction is suspended over this wretched race, and that the hand of providence is removing them to give place to a people more worthy of this beautiful and fertile country, we arrived at the place of our encampment, and found ourselves again on the great California trail.[35]

In 1841 a noteworthy expedition of a different character explored the Rogue country. Lieutenant Charles Wilkes, commander of the United States South Seas Surveying and Exploring Expedition, ordered a detachment under George F. Emmons to explore a land route between the Columbia and San Francisco Bay. Several soldiers, four seamen, an artist, a geologist, a naturalist, a surgeon, two botanists, guides, and hunters, including an Iroquois Indian, and the first white women to travel by land between Oregon and California made up the party of thirty-nine.[36] The published diaries of George M. Colvocoresses, William Dunlop Brackenridge, and Titian Ramsey Peale, the reminiscent account of Joel P. Walker, and the manuscript journals of Henry Eld and George F. Emmons vividly document their journey.

In September the expedition crossed the Umpqua Mountains. On the twenty-seventh it passed Rocky Point, and Calvin Tibbets, one of the hunters, told the party that he had been attacked there twice. The men saw many Indians on the opposite bank of the river, and the Rogues, no doubt as

[35] *Ibid.*, 117–18.
[36] Colvocoresses, *Four Years in a Government Exploring Expedition*, 371.

curious as the explorers, followed the travelers. Advancing through the hills near present Gold Hill, Peale wrote: "Our course was nearly N E up Rogues river for about two hours, when we struck off through a pass in the mountains, and reached extensive plaines, where we saw three *mountd* Ind[ns] who fled on our approach."[37]

The usual trail malady, fever and chills, incapacitated several of the men on the twenty-eighth. Colvocoresses became so delirious that his gun had to be taken from him. On this day, one warm enough to scorch the poison oak leaves to a bright red and to dry the grass to straw, near the sulphur spring at present Ashland, Peale wrote the first image-evoking description of one of the aboriginal inhabitants of the Rogue River Valley:

> Indian signs were numerous, though we saw but one, a squaw who was so busy setting fire to the prairie & mountain ravines that she seemed to disregard us; her dress was a mantle of antelope or deer skin, and cup shaped cap, made of rushes. She had a large funnel shaped basket which they *all* carry to collect roots and seeds in.[38]

With some concern the expedition left Bear Creek and began the climb over the Siskiyous. The tales of massacre along this trail and the weakened condition of the men forced them to be vigilant. All went well, however, and on the afternoon of September 29 the party reached the summit. To its right the coast mountains were ablaze in an unchecked forest fire, and to the south were the snow-covered slopes of Mount Shasta. A twenty-mile ride brought the explorers to the Klamath River and into California.[39]

Two years later, in 1843, Joel P. Walker, whose family had journeyed to California with the Emmons expedition, returned to Oregon driving twelve hundred cattle, two hun-

[37] Jessie Poesch, *Titian Ramsay Peale, 1799–1885, and His Journals of the Wilkes Expedition*, 192.
[38] *Ibid.*
[39] *Ibid.*, 192–93.

dred horses, and six hundred sheep.[40] Possibly it was the Walker party that Lansford W. Hastings met in the Rogue River valley that June. Hastings and fifty-two others were headed for California, but when they met the cattle drovers, nearly half of the men turned back for Oregon. Hastings stated that the Rogues assisted his party in crossing the Rogue River, but that the Shastas attacked his men when they were camped on the Klamath.[41]

Walker passed on sage advice about his experiences on the Oregon-California trail to mountain man James Clyman. On one of the front pages of his 1845 journal, Clyman quoted Walker's admonition: "Never Fire a gun after (after) crossing the Umpqua mountain untill you cross the siskiew mountain perhaps Five day travel Keep yourselves close as possible in traveling through the brush."[42]

Clyman's party contained thirty-five men, one woman, and three children. One of the travelers was James W. Marshall, who discovered gold three years later at Sutter's Mill on the American River.[43] The expedition reached the Rogue, or "Clamet" as Clyman called it, on June 20, 1845. Several Indians attempted to enter the camp but were kept at a distance. They serenaded the party with war songs the whole night. On June 22 the expedition entered the Rogue Valley and was greatly impressed by snow-capped Mount McLoughlin to the east. Clyman surveyed Table Rock, the monolithic lava ledge dominating the lower part of the valley, and correctly assumed that the Indians used it as "a place of safety in seasons of danger." The men passed up Bear Creek, climbed

[40] Joel P. Walker, *A Pioneer of Pioneers: Narrative of Adventure thro' Alabama, Florida, New Mexico, Oregon & California, etc.*, 15.
[41] Lansford W. Hastings, *The Emigrant's Guide to Oregon and California*, 64–67.
[42] *James Clyman, Frontiersman: The Adventures of a Trapper and Covered-Wagon Emigrant as Told in His Own Reminiscences and Diaries*, 161–62.
[43] LeRoy R. Hafen (ed.), *The Mountain Men and the Fur Trade of the Far West*, I, 249.

the Siskiyous, and as Clyman expressed it, "soon had a view of the country from the summit which was wild and awfully sublime."[44]

In 1846 a steady and increasing stream of travelers crossed through the Rogue country. The supply of furs was diminishing, but another attraction, the lure of Oregon land, brought the new influx of people. In June, Jesse and Lindsay Applegate, Levi Scott, and a dozen other residents of the Willamette Valley left their homes to open a wagon route that would avoid the treacherous Snake River section of the Oregon Trail and the difficult journey from The Dalles of the Columbia to the Willamette.

Along the South Umpqua River the Applegate expedition found the first signs of Indian troubles. The trail was littered with broken arrows and signs of a battle that had been fought between travelers and the Umpquas.[45] When the party was in the mountains near Grave Creek, the Indians dashed from tree to tree on the ridges above it, and at the Rogue River they boldly followed the explorers along the opposite bank. The Rogues contested nearly every foray into their domain. When they did not attack travelers, they often managed to spirit away stray horses and mules.[46]

Rather than taking the usual trail over the Siskiyous to the Klamath River, the Applegates and their companions opened the Green Springs passage from the Rogue Valley over the Cascades to Klamath Lake. They reached Fort Hall and persuaded a number of immigrants to follow them to Oregon. In August, ninety or one hundred wagons left the Oregon Trail bound for the Willamette on the Southern Emigrant Route or Applegate Cutoff. They were guided by Scott and David Goff while the Applegates and others went ahead to cut brush and open the way. The first immigrants reached the

[44] *James Clyman, Frontiersman*, 162.

[45] Lindsay Applegate, "Notes and Reminiscences of Laying out and Establishing the Old Emigrant Road into Southern Oregon in the Year 1846," *Oregon Historical Quarterly*, Vol. XXII, No. 1 (1921), 16–17.

[46] *Ibid.*, 19–20.

Rogue Valley on October 9, but stragglers were days behind this group. Some wagons lingered too long in the valley; by the time they attempted to cross the Umpqua Mountains the rains had begun. Twisting Canyon Creek, the only possible trail, was thick with boulders, fallen timber, and chaparral. Lack of food and destruction of wagons added to the misery.[47]

Throughout November and December the Willamette Valley settlers sent food and assistance to the immigrants stranded on the trail. Starvation and sickness took a heavy toll. Martha Crowley perished near the banks of a small stream in the Umpqua Mountains that carries a reminder of her death—it is called Grave Creek. The second week in November, one of the stragglers, John Newton, was murdered by the Umpqua Indians as he lay in his tent too helpless to fight back.[48] Nearly a dozen families remained in the Umpqua Valley until January, 1847. Some took refuge at the Hudson's Bay Company post at the mouth of Elk Creek.[49]

As each party encountered the rascally behavior of the Indians in the Rogue country, the residents of Oregon grew more resentful and hostile to the aboriginal people. Even pioneers who had only heard of the difficulties held to the frontier maxim—at least, when it applied to the Rogues—that the only good Indians were dead ones. This attitude was well reflected in a letter of advice written in April, 1847, by Charles G. Pickett for the *Oregon Spectator*:

Treat the Indians along the road kindly, but trust them not. After you get to the Siskiyou Mountains, use your pleasure in spilling blood, but were I traveling with you, from this on to the first sight of the Sacramento Valley my only communication with these treacherous, cowardly, untamable rascals would be through my rifle. The character of their country precludes the idea of making peace with them, or ever maintaining treaties if made; so that

---

[47] Bancroft, *History of Oregon, 1834–1848*, 557–59.
[48] Walter Meacham, *Applegate Trail*, 15–16, 21. John Minto, "Early Days of Oregon" (MS), 39.
[49] Bancroft, *History of Oregon, 1834–1848*, 565.

philanthropy must be set aside in cases of necessity, while self-preservation here dictates these savages being killed off as soon as possible.[50]

Counsel of this nature, especially when it was from the man who was appointed Oregon's first Indian agent, added to the ill will. The outbreak of the Cayuse War in northern Oregon in 1847 further fired the animosities toward the Indians.

Troubles brewed again in the Rogue Valley. In spite of the hardships suffered by the pioneers of 1846, the advocates of the Applegate Trail were certain that they had discovered a practical route to Oregon. Thus in May, 1847, Levi Scott led twenty men over the trail and that fall guided twenty-five wagons from Fort Hall to the Willamette Valley. As usual the Rogues attacked the immigrants.[51]

In the spring of 1848 a company of six men led by John Saxton attempted to drive one hundred head of horses to California. Before they had reached the Klamath River, the Indians had killed or stolen sixty-five of the herd.[52]

Throughout these years of intermittent hostilities in the Rogue Valley, the people living on the southwest Oregon coast remained peaceful. However, in September, 1849, a pilot ship, the *William G. Hagstaff*, sailing from San Francisco to the Columbia River, attempted to enter the Rogue. The ship went aground and was stormed by the Indians, who plundered and burned the vessel. The captain, Charles White, and eighteen men aboard it escaped into the mountains and wandered for nearly three weeks until they arived at Fort Umpqua.[53]

The booming speculation and exploration that followed the discovery of gold in California led others to the shores

[50] April 29, 1847.

[51] T. L. Davidson, "By the Southern Route into Oregon" (MS), 2–6.

[52] *Oregon Spectator*, May 4, 1848.

[53] Hubert Howe Bancroft, *History of Oregon: 1848–1888*, 191. L[orin] L. Williams, "First Settlements in Southwestern Oregon. T'Vault's Expedition" (MS), 2. George Davidson, *Pacific Coast: Coast Pilot of California, Oregon, and Washington Territory*, 112.

of southern Oregon. One party, a company of seventy men organized by Herman Winchester in San Francisco, sailed to the mouth of Rogue River on the *Samuel Roberts* in the spring of 1850. The explorers lowered a skiff off the bar and waited to see if their big vessel might cross in. The launch overturned in the breakers. Two men drowned, and the Indians immediately surrounded the four who swam to shore and stripped them of their clothing.[54] The schooner, after several tacks, plunged through the rough surf and entered the calmer waters of the river. An armed party rescued the naked explorers while detachments ventured along the coast both north and south and others rowed up river. One group clambered up Elephant Rock, a monolith below the large Tututni village at Edson Creek, and chiseled the initials of the schooner and the date on the rock face.[55]

The Indians often surrounded the *Roberts* in their canoes during the days that she lay in the harbor. Sometimes the captain permitted the visitors to come on board, but when their thieving became too annoying, they were ordered to stay off. The Indians then attempted to remove the copper plates protecting the ship's hull; one particularly ambitious man vainly sawed at the anchor chain. One morning when an unusually large number of warriors paddled down river toward the ship, the explorers feared an attack. As the canoes drew into close range, the men fired a blank charge from their cannon. The echo resounded from the hills, and, when the smoke first cleared, they saw only empty canoes resting placidly in the river. Timidly, the Indians bobbed to the surface and swam for shore.[56]

The Winchester party sailed north along the coast and on August 4 entered the Umpqua River. The men proceeded

---

[54] Bancroft, *History of Oregon: 1848–1888*, 176–78. C. T. H[opkins], "An Exploring Expedition in 1850," *Overland Monthly* (2d Series), Vol. XVII, No. 101 (1891), 476–77.

[55] H[opkins], "An Exploring Expedition in 1850," *loc. cit.*

[56] *Ibid.*

to the head of tidewater, hiked along the forested riverbanks to Fort Umpqua, and located several townsites.[57]

While the San Francisco speculators were on the coast, new events occurred in the valley. Near Rocky Point the Rogues attacked miners returning from California. When the men fled into the brush, the Indians plundered the camp and stole several pouches of gold dust. As soon as the angry miners reached the Willamette Valley, they requested the territorial governor, Joseph Lane, to help them recover their gold.[58]

In June, Lane enlisted about fifteen men to go to the Rogue River, initiating the first Oregon government action toward the Indians of that region. Quatley, a Klicitat chief from the central part of Oregon Territory, and ten of his people accompanied the expedition. Lane hoped to assemble the Indians of the Rogue Valley, recover the stolen gold, and draw up a treaty. He took "cheap presents" to conclude the negotiations.[59]

Two days after arriving in the valley, Lane held a conference which drew seventy-five or one hundred Indians. The people who assembled were primarily the fierce Latgawas from the upper reaches of the river, but a few of the Takelmas also came in. The meeting had hardly comenced when another seventy-five warriors, well armed with bows, arrows, and about twenty guns, came marching down the river to the conference grounds. Lane's men acted quickly. They surrounded the headman, "Joe," the spokesman for the Rogues. At this juncture, the newcomers joined the circle and listened to the proceedings.[60]

Lane paced up and down, speaking, reminding, gesticulating, and carrying each point as best he could. He spoke in

[57] A. Lyman, "How the Schooner *Samuel Roberts* entered the Umpqua River on Sunday, August 4, 1850" (undated clipping from the Roseburg *Plaindealer* in the possession of Harold A. Minter, Portland, Ore.). Addison C. Gibbs, "Notes on the History of Oregon" (MS), 5.
[58] Joseph Lane, "Autobiography" (MS), 88–89.
[59] *Ibid.*, 89.
[60] *Ibid.*, 91–92.

brief thrusts, for each statement was translated for his listeners. He reminded the Rogues of their incessant attacks on passing parties. Further, he insisted that they must return all property stolen since the jurisdiction of the United States was extended over their domain. He told the Indians that above all they must turn over the gold which they had recently seized. He coupled his demands with the assurance that the Rogues would be protected if they acceded to his requests.[61]

The headman, "Joe," stood up. He gazed at his men, looked across the deep flowing river, and suddenly spoke loudly and sharply. He had uttered not more than a few sentences when his warriors leaped to their feet with wild yells. In the tumult "Joe" ran from the circle but was seized by the Klicitats, who threw him to the ground and placed a knife to his throat. Their leader helpless, the warriors quieted down and heard him beg them to disperse. "Joe," at the prompting of his captors, ordered his men to reassemble in two days, "in good humor."

The hours passed, and Lane became better acquainted with his prisoner. In their conversations, Lane promised that if an agreement was concluded, he could obtain a permanent agent to reside in the region. Each year that the peace was maintained, the government would distribute gifts to "Joe's" people.[62]

At the allotted time a number of warriors returned to Lane's camp bringing several stolen items. The Indians did not have the gold dust. They told Lane that they did not know the coarse gold bits and flakes were of any value. They had wanted the fine pouches and had poured the gold into the river. In spite of the failure of this part of his mission, Lane concluded a provisional agreement with the assembled men. With this act his official service as governor of Oregon Territory and ex officio superintendent of Indians affairs ended. Since the new appointee was expected momentarily and the

[61] *Ibid.*, 92.
[62] *Ibid.*, 93–96.

gold fields of California were alluringly near, the Lane party continued south on the trail.[63]

As the men rode out of the valley and climbed through the pines on the slopes of the Siskiyous, the changes that had come to the Rogue country were evident. This realm of the Indians was no longer unknown and unvisited. It had yielded to the fur trapper and the cattle drover. The solitude of the hills and shore was broken by the thundering cannons, creaking wheels, and lusty yells of the newcomers.

[63] *Ibid.*, 101.

3

CONFLICTS AND CLASHES

IN SPITE OF the penetration of their homeland, the Rogues changed little in their life and outlook. They bartered for trinkets and metal with the Hudson's Bay Company traders, but they continued to use bows, arrows, stone knives, and bark and skin clothing. Although the white men who entered their homeland found a fierce and proud people, not every expedition suffered at their hands. Year after year John McLoughlin reported to his superiors in London that all was peaceful for the southern brigades. The explosions of violence in southwest Oregon were brief and few until 1851. That year the Indians felt more keenly than ever before that a contest was developing over control of the Rogue country.

Gold lured new men into the region. Prospectors camped in the ravines and panned the creek bottoms south of the Siskiyous while others approached the region from the north. In January a party of seventeen struggled through the Umpqua Mountains with wagons and pack animals. As had happened before, the Rogues harassed these explorers.

When the miners reached the Rogue River, they met Indians who volunteered to lead them to a region rich in gold. Several of the men, including James A. Cardwell, who recorded their adventures, left their pack animals with a guard and followed the Indians to the mouth of the Applegate River. Here they discovered a large, deserted village. The guides, members of the band who lived on Grave Creek, encouraged the Indians to come from their hiding places in the surrounding hills.

Some of these people joined the prospectors; the expedition went up the Applegate some six miles to camp on an open prairie. The miners found color, but could continue the search only cautiously, for, as Cardwell recalled, "the indians began to show themselves in large numbers on the hills above us and they would yell horribly and roll stones down as if to try to frighten us away."[1]

The next night, camped farther up the river, the men became so uneasy and fearful of an attack that after dark they packed and crossed the hills to the Rogue. In the morning they discovered that they were about a mile downstream from the cabin of Joel Perkins, the operator of a ferry and one of the earliest settlers along the river.[2]

Deciding not to spend more time in this region, the prospectors turned south to try their luck in California. On March 12 they discovered gold in a small basinlike valley on the Shasta River, a tributary of the Klamath.[3] The wealth of the area had first been tapped when a miner named Dollarhide found gold on Beaver Creek in June, 1850. The Indians drove Dollarhide from his claim, but soon thereafter a larger party worked the gravel bars of this stream and called it Scott River.[4]

The discovery of gold on the Shasta initiated a rush that drew thousands of men into northern California. These miners, moving into a land well populated by the Indians, struck against them at the slightest provocation. Their vengeance was not confined to California.

In May the Indians attacked three packers camping on

[1] James A. Cardwell, "Emigrant Company" (MS), 8.

[2] Perkins' Ferry, near present Grants Pass, was subsequently known as Long's, then Vannoy's Ferry. *Ibid.*, 9–10. L. J. C. Duncan, "Settlement in Southern Oregon" (MS), 3–6.

[3] Cardwell, "Emigrant Company," *loc. cit.*, 10.

[4] U.S. Congress, House, *House Misc. Doc. No. 47*, 35 Cong., 2 sess., 44.

Bear Creek south of the Rogue River ford. When the two survivors reached the mines at Yreka, a company of volunteers formed to avenge the murder. The miners rode into the Rogue Valley, shot two Indians, and seized two men and two women as hostages.[5]

The miners, in retaliation for the murder of two prospectors in early May, next attacked the Shastas living near the diggings at Yreka. The volunteers also struck several rancherias in Scott Valley. They indiscriminately killed men, women, and children as they burned the Indian houses in their predawn attacks. Still not satisfied with their campaign of destruction, the volunteers cut through the mountains for the coast of northern California to the valley of the Smith River, at whose mouth Jedediah Smith had camped in 1828.[6]

They rode over old Indian trails into a land as yet untouched by miners. As the volunteers crossed the mountains, they looked into the verdant valley of the Smith River. Along the banks of the stream were virgin stands of redwoods. To the west was a heavy fog bank. As the party wandered through the forest, the men discussed their plans. J. B. Long, their leader, announced that his goal was to whip into subjugation the Indians along this river. His men, adopting this resolution, found a Tolowa village of about nine lodges. To their surprise, many of the Indians were armed with rifles and Hudson's Bay Company guns. Long insisted on taking away the weapons of these peaceful people. A stolen rifle and mutual distrust heightened the tensions in the village, and when the Indians captured Long, who had walked into their midst to demand their surrender, the two parties seized their weapons and fought for nearly an hour. The ten white men battled thirty Indians. Four of the latter were killed, and several were wounded. On the morning of June 8, Long and his boastful

[5] The Rogues had killed David Dilley near present Phoenix. *Oregon Statesman*, June 20, 1851.

[6] *Alta California*, July 3, 1851.

company left the valley to again cross the Siskiyous to the Rogue.[7]

These acts of the volunteers, which far exceeded the hostilities of the Indians, roused the Shastas to retaliate. On June 17 they attacked the pack train of Ford, Penny, Homan & Company between Indian Creek and the Scott River on the south side of the Klamath. They murdered three of the packers.[8]

A series of troubles had also occurred in the Rogue Valley during the first weeks of June. Twenty-six men were ambushed on June 1 twenty miles south of the Rogue River ford. They killed one Indian and escaped. The next day the Rogues attacked four miners at the same place. Although robbed of their packs and animals, the men retreated in safety to Perkins' Ferry. The same day the Indians fired on a pack train owned by I. B. Nichols and wounded one man. They killed four travelers in another party in an ambush.[9]

On the evening of June 2 a four-hour battle occurred at the ambush site on Bear Creek after the Rogues attacked thirty-two miners returning from California under the leadership of Dr. James McBride. Even though they had initiated the troubles, the Rogues lost seven men and had several wounded. They injured only one miner, but they spirited away horses with packs containing an estimated fifteen hundred dollars in supplies and gold dust.[10]

News of these bloody encounters on both the Rogue and the Klamath was carried quickly to the north. On June 13, Joseph Lane, who lived on the Umpqua River at Winchester, one of the townsites laid out by the explorers from the *Samuel Roberts* the previous year, wrote to John P. Gaines, governor

[7] *Ibid.*

[8] William Mosier, Keever (or McKeever), and a man named Amos were killed. Reportedly the Indians stole $6,000 worth of supplies. U.S. Congress, Senate, *Senate Exec. Doc. No. 4*, 33 Cong., special sess., 276–77.

[9] *Oregon Statesman*, June 20, 1851. George W. Riddle, *Early Days in Oregon: A History of the Riddle Valley*, 55.

[10] *Oregon Statesman*, June 20, 1851.

of Oregon Territory. Referring to the Indians, he complained: "They will cut off our trade with the mines, kill many of the whites traveling in that direction, and seriously injure the prospects and interests of the people of this Territory." Lane also mentioned that he was considering raising a company of volunteers to go to the Rogue to make peace as he had done the year before.[11]

Before Lane could act, Major Philip Kearny, with twenty-eight United States troops, entered the valley on an overland trip to San Francisco. The only government forces that had passed through the region prior to these men were those in the Emmons party of 1841 and some venturesome deserters pursued to the Klamath River by Colonel William Loring in the spring of 1850.[12] On June 17, in the valley a few miles up the Rogue River from Table Rock, the Indians attacked Kearny's detachment. They mortally wounded Captain James Stuart, a veteran of the Mexican War, and injured two other men.[13] The Rogues lost at least seventeen warriors in the battle.[14]

Kearny, determined to defeat the Indians, sent to Yreka for reinforcements. In the meantime Lane had enlisted a small company of volunteers and was on his way south when he learned of the bloody encounter. Urging his men to hurry, he arrived in the valley on June 22 but was unable to locate Kearny's base camp until the following day. The government troops fought skirmishes on the twenty-third; one of their

[11] U.S. Congress, House, *House Exec. Doc. No. 2*, 32 Cong., 1 sess., 145–46.

[12] Colonel Loring saw his command dwindle after he arrived in Oregon Territory in 1849. The gold fields of California were a magnet for his men. In March, 1850, with thirteen officers and eighty troops, Loring set out to capture deserters. He overtook fifty-six men in the Umpqua Valley and captured seventeen more on the Klamath River. Raymond W. Settle (ed.), *The March of the Mounted Riflemen*, 21–22.

[13] Francis B. Heitman, *Historical Register and Dictionary of the United States Army, From Its Organization, September 29, 1789, to March 2, 1903*, I, 933.

[14] *Oregon Statesman*, July 4, 1851. *Alta California*, July 16, 1851.

51

battles lasted for over four hours and stopped only when the Indians escaped in the darkness. After Lane and Kearny joined forces, they searched along the river. They fought one battle on the twenty-fifth and ended the campaign the next day, directing their forces to assemble at newly named Camp Stewart near present Phoenix. Lane estimated that during the ten days of warfare at least fifty Indians had been killed or wounded.[15]

Lane set out immediately for the mines at Yreka. By the time Governor Gaines of Oregon came hurrying south to the Rogue Valley with a small group of men, Kearny had also departed, taking with him about thirty Indian women and children as prisoners. Gaines, much ridiculed in the territorial newspapers for his expedition, was unable to induce Kearny to return to the Rogue. However, when Lane had finished his business in California and learned that Kearny was camped nearby with the prisoners, he offered to return the Indians to the Rogue Valley and place them in the governor's custody.[16]

On July 7 he delivered the hostages to Gaines and his fifteen-man force. The governor then initiated negotiations, and the Indians renewed their 1850 promise to return stolen property and stop attacking travelers. To seal the agreement the white men gave fifteen or twenty blankets, some pipes, a keg of tobacco, and a promise to return items they had stolen from the Indians.[17]

With peace secured in the Rogue Valley, miners cautiously spied out serpentine outcroppings, hunched with pan in hand along the little creeks of the Siskiyous, and searched, always hoping, for wealth. That summer of 1851 was also the beginning of a new era for the Indians who lived near the sea.

The boom of California in the 1850's brought a lively trade in produce, mail, and passengers to the Pacific coast. Steamers and sailing ships connected Panama and San Fran-

---

[15] *Oregon Statesman*, July 4, 22, 1851.
[16] *Ibid.*, July 22, 29, 1851.
[17] *Ibid.*

cisco, San Francisco and Portland, Portland and the Hawaiian Islands. By 1851 one of these small steamers, a one-stack vessel named the *Sea Gull*, was a regular on the San Francisco–Portland route.[18] Captain William Tichenor of the *Sea Gull*, sailing for miles along the unsettled coasts of northern California and southern Oregon, saw that a shipping port somewhere in that region, a port that would serve as a base for the pack trains to carry supplies to the mining camps on the upper Klamath River, would be a profitable undertaking. In late May, Tichenor hired a crew of nine men in Portland to be the landing party and founders of a town that he hoped to establish at Port Orford.[19]

On the morning of June 9 the *Sea Gull* passed the reef and scattered rocks off Cape Blanco and a few miles to the south turned into the harbor of Port Orford. Before the landing party rowed ashore in a launch, Tichenor assured the men that they did not need to worry about the Indians. To make them feel more secure, however, he augmented their guns with "three old flint lock muskets, one old sword that was half eaten with rust and a few pounds of lead and three or four pounds of powder."[20] When the boat reached the beach, the men saw only a few Indians on the nearby cliffs. These members of the Quotomah band were probably descendants of those Indians who visited Vancouver in 1792. Now, in 1851, they did not appear so friendly.

The landing party did not like the situation, but when Captain Tichenor sent an old cannon ashore, they decided to stay. These nine men were to lay out a townsite, search for a trail into the mountains, and await the arrival of more men,

[18] Orvil Dodge, *Pioneer History of Coos and Curry Counties, Oregon*, 21–22.
[19] Those in Tichenor's employ were J. M. Kirkpatrick, J. H. Eagan, John T. Slater, George Ridoubt, T. D. Palmer, Joseph Hussey, Cyrus W. Hedden, James Carrigan, and Jacob Summers. Kirkpatrick, the leader, wrote two accounts of their adventures. *Alta California*, July 25, 1851. J. M. Kirkpatrick, *The Heroes of Battle Rock, or The Miners Reward*.
[20] Kirkpatrick, *The Heroes of Battle Rock*, 2.

arms, and supplies which the *Sea Gull* was to bring in fourteen days. As the small steamer sailed for San Francisco, the men packed their provisions and arms up the beach and made camp among the pines atop what is today known as Battle Rock. The Indians, some of whom lived in a village a few hundred feet away on a stream later known as Gold Run, retreated down the beach to a village on Hubbard Creek.

That first night on the southwest Oregon coast, the party loaded their weapons and prepared for trouble if it should come. J. M. Kirkpatrick described the loading of the cannon:

> We put in a two pound sack of powder and on top of that about half of an old cotton shirt and then on top of that as much bar lead cut up in pieces of from one to two inches in length as I could hold in my two hands, then a couple of old newspapers on top. We then primed the gun with some fine rifle powder and trained it so as to rake the narrow ridge in front of the muzzle.[21]

At dawn the next morning the Indians gathered on the cliffs and held a war dance. Soon they were shooting arrows at the rock, but they did not advance until about midmorning, when a large canoe containing twelve men arrived from the south. Among these warriors was a tall man wearing a red shirt.

The distinctively clad leader drew a long knife, waved it above his head, yelled threateningly, and marched down the beach toward the rock with nearly one hundred men. The Indians surged over the tidal flat between Battle Rock and the shore and rushed madly up the ledge toward the camp. Kirkpatrick lit a tarred rope, and when the leader of the attack was no more than a few feet from the rampart, he thrust it into the priming. A thunderous blast exploded into the midst of the Indians.

The cannon flew backward in recoil, and the white men knew at once they had no time for a second shot. The defenders of Battle Rock rushed into the smoke among the dying In-

21 *Ibid.*, 3.

dians, screaming, shooting, and driving the survivors onto the beach. When their opponents had retreated, the white men counted seventeen bodies about their perch and knew that many more men were seriously wounded. Two of Kirkpatrick's party were struck by arrows during the battle.[22]

For several hours all was quiet at the harbor of Port Orford; then a single Indian appeared. He walked down the beach toward the rock, laid down his bow, arrows, and knife, and appeared ready to talk with the defenders of Battle Rock. Kirkpatrick attempted to explain that the *Sea Gull* would return in thirteen days for his party. The Indian sought permission to remove the bodies.

He carried away all of the dead Indians except for the man in the red shirt. When Kirkpatrick attempted to get him to remove the fallen leader, the Indian shook his head, stooped down and tore the dead man's shirt, gave the body a kick, and walked away. Kirkpatrick buried this man, an "Indian" with blond hair and freckles. He was later believed to have been the survivor of a Russian ship wrecked on the coast several years before.[23]

For the next two weeks the nine men, continually watched by the Indians, remained in their camp. They killed one Indian when he fired on the men repairing the earth rampart on the rock. On the fifteenth day, when the *Sea Gull* failed to return, the Rogues again gathered on the beach. While they danced, other warriors appeared from the north and from the south. Then the armed Indians turned toward the party on the pine-covered island. When the leader of the Rogues shouted across the water, the nine men decided that perhaps they should try to kill this headman as well.

As the Indians, armed with their bows and slender arrows tipped with finely worked points of flint, jasper, or obsidian, advanced across the beach, Kirkpatrick and James Carrigan fired. The leader fell; his compatriots, uttering piercing cries,

[22] *Ibid.,* 3–4.
[23] *Ibid.,* 5.

turned and carried away his body. An hour later Kirkpatrick repelled a second attack in the same way. With the loss of another headman, the Indians retreated down the shore, but, to the worry of the men on the rock, numerous canoes came into sight from the south. Fearing a night attack, the party carefully considered its position—ocean on one side, forest and hostile Indians on the other, and only six rounds of ammunition to each man. Deciding to make a show of strengthening their defenses, they chopped down a tree, raised the rampart, and watched the shore. While the men worked, they counted over a hundred Indians leaving the cliffs and going to the village at Hubbard Creek.

Late in the day, when they believed they were unguarded, the nine men scrambled down the rocky ledge, leaving tents, blankets, the cannon, and provisions which they could not carry, and dashed for the forest. They hurried along, hoping to get some distance before dark, but a few miles from Port Orford they ran directly into a band of thirty Indians coming south on the trail. When the nine yelled and charged, the Indians scattered.

At sunset, and fortunately at low tide, the escaping party crossed the Elk River, a stream entering the ocean just to the south of Cape Blanco. They continued on all night, breaking their way through the thick growth of spruce, huckleberry, alder, and pine growing near the ocean. At midafternoon the following day they entered a swamp, probably near Floras or New Lake. For hours they floundered in the tangle of logs, water, and darkness until they took refuge on a small island. Their rest was brief: the mosquitoes and fear of the Indians drove them on.

The next morning they again followed the beach and discovered that many Indians were ahead of them, but when the tracks turned up a small stream, the nine were again ahead of their pursuers. Late in the afternoon they reached the southern shore of the Coquille River. As Jedediah Smith had looked across and seen the villages among the pines and sand dunes to the north, these men also noted many Indians on the far shore. Perhaps two hundred warriors, so Kirkpatrick recalled, awaited them. The refugees quickly decided to travel along the south side of the river, and, if possible, go through the mountains to the Oregon–California trail.

As they proceeded upstream, the Indians followed on the opposite bank. Some four miles from the mouth of the river, probably between Prosper and Parkersburg, the nine men climbed a hillside. Looking across the valley, they saw the Coquilles crossing the river in their canoes. The weary men plunged into the brush and, when well hidden, tumbled into a sinkhole filled with grass and sedge. Although they were hungry and worried about their pursuers, the nine were soon fast asleep.[24]

The next morning, shrouded in a heavy fog, they returned to the river, collected driftwood, and built a raft to carry the guns and the three men who could not swim. When all was ready, six of the party plunged into the cold water and pulled the raft toward the north shore of the Coquille. Reaching a muddy bank, they unfastened the ropes, left the logs to float away, and continued their journey; however, within a few hundred feet the men discovered that they were on an island—Carlson's Island at present Randolph.

George Ridoubt swam to the north shore and began to chop down a pine tree which he hoped the nonswimmers might use as a float for crossing the last part of the river. While he was at work, a canoe with three Indians came around the bend. The Coquilles were so absorbed in watching the white man that they did not see the other eight in the party. Only when in rifle range did the Indians discover that they were not alone. Leveled guns persuaded them to come to the island.

Just as the sun worked through the morning fog, the eight men crowded into the canoe and paddled to the north bank of the river. The party abandoned its attempt to go east through the mountains and pushed on all day through the

24 *Ibid.*, 10.

forest. That night the men slept in the solitude of the spruce and pine. Early the next morning they found the beach again at Whiskey Run, a small creek and later a famous gold field about ten miles north of the Coquille. The hungry men gathered mussels from the rocks that made up a broken reef and small headland just north of the creek. They were trying to cook their meal when an Indian—one who had been in the canoe the previous day—approached them speaking jargon, the trade language used by Indians and traders along several hundred miles of the Pacific coast. He told them that they must hurry on, for the Coquille Indians were coming up the beach in search of them.

So the weary men, clutching handfuls of raw mussels, continued their retreat to the north, accompanied by their new Indian friend. In midafternoon the refugees passed a white pole some twenty feet high standing in a pile of rocks near the beach. Their traveling companion told them that there was now no need for worry; the pole marked the boundary of the Coos Indians, and the Coquilles would not dare venture beyond it.[25]

The Indians at Coos Bay received the Kirkpatrick party with kindness, gave the men food, and took them across the harbor. The men continued on through the swamps and sand dunes and along the beach trail to the north. At sunset on July 2, the hungry, wounded, and tattered refugees from Battle Rock reached the southern shore of the Umpqua River. The few white men who lived at newly established Umpqua City, a small and never-thriving town on the sand spit north of the river's mouth, paddled across the stream to rescue them.[26]

During the days that the defenders of Battle Rock had laboriously retreated north along the coast, Captain Tichenor had been unable to leave San Francisco. He was deeply in debt when he arrived there, and creditors had seized his ship.[27]

[25] *Ibid.*, 12.
[26] *Ibid.*, 13.
[27] *Ibid.*, 15.

The steamer *Columbia* of the Pacific Navigation Company departed a day early to go to Port Orford to find the nine men. When the *Columbia* arrived at the harbor, all was quiet. A shore party found only the body of the man buried on the beach (but since disinterred by the waves), the signs of battle, and an inscription on a stump which said, "Look Beneath." When they dug in the fresh earth, they found a small daily entry journal which Kirkpatrick had kept as a record of the days of waiting for rescue. His notations about the diminishing ammunition and food and the hostility of the Indians led the men on the *Columbia* to believe that all had been killed. When the nine men eventually reached the Willamette Valley, they read in the Oregon newspapers about their deaths at Port Orford.[28]

While the refugees were fleeing from Battle Rock and Governor Gaines was fuming and worrying about a treaty in the Rogue River valley, Captain Tichenor straightened out his finances. About the second week of July, he left San Francisco with a more fully equipped expedition for a second attempt to settle Port Orford. The *Sea Gull* brought seventy armed men, four cannons, and provisions to establish a settlement financed by four or five proprietors. The men built two stockades and mounted the cannon. When their enlistment expired, they began prospecting, sawing lumber, and making shingles from the newly discovered, fine-grained Port Orford cedar. They kept a guard posted each night. According to one of the men, the curious Indians were "warmly treated." At least one was wounded.[29]

Port Orford had been established only a few weeks when William G. T'Vault, a guide for Kearny in the Rogue Valley, arrived to lead the exploration party that hoped to open a road from the coast to the Oregon–California trail. The Port Orford promoters thought that the distance would be less than fifty miles and that finding a trail would make Port Orford a

[28] *Ibid.*
[29] *Alta California*, Aug. 1, 26, 1851.

harbor of great importance. T'Vault, described in a letter from Port Orford in August "as being every way qualified to conduct a party in an enterprise of this character," set out on August 24 with twenty-three men.[30]

The men journeyed for three days down the coast until they reached the mouth of the Rogue River. As they followed the black sand beaches, growing numbers of Indians pursued them. The Rogues, muscular, bronzed, and alarmed by these new intruders in their homeland, moved closer and closer to the exploring party. The men from Port Orford quickly decided to try to outdistance them and turned up the north side of the river. The rugged terrain slowed their progress, and the presence of the Indians was a constant worry.

Hoping to prevent ambush, the explorers carefully burned the grass around their camps when they stopped for the night on meadows near the river. Each day the trail became more difficult, and understandably so, for the Mikonotunnes and the Tututni who lived in the area customarily used canoes to pass through especially rugged terrain like that at Copper Canyon. At last, when nearly all food was exhausted and T'Vault was unable to recognize any landmarks of the Oregon–California trail, thirteen men turned back for Port Orford.[31]

T'Vault convinced nine others to continue the search, but by September 7 they were lost and starving. Game was scarce, and they spent several evenings discussing the prospects of living on horseflesh. Finally the men arrived at the Big Bend of the Rogue, and although T'Vault expected the road to California to be around the next turn in the river, his men refused to travel farther. Two of the party, weakened by the rugged trip and lack of food, lay down to die; they were restored to traveling condition when one of the men killed an elk, which made a welcome feast for the explorers.

30 *Ibid.*, Aug. 26, 1851. Frances Fuller Victor, *The Early Indian Wars of Oregon*, 282–83.
31 Williams, "First Settlements in Southwestern Oregon," *loc. cit.*, 14–17.

In spite of this temporary relief, their situation was desperate. Lorin L. Williams, a member of the expedition, wrote:

We again set out an in about one or two miles, we came upon an old, but a plain and well beaten Indian trail leading from Rogue River on the right, directly across our route in a course about N.N.W. T'Vault explained to the men, that the Hudson Bay Company had a trading post on the Umpqua River, some 50 or 60 miles from its mouth; that good trail run south from there through the Mountains to a point on Rogue River; that the Indians from Rogue River passed over said trail in large numbers upon their annual trading expeditions to the fort.[32]

Thus hoping to find their way through the mountains to Fort Umpqua, the explorers left the Rogue near its Big Bend and guided their horses over the madroña, oak, and fir-covered mountains to the watershed of a river to the north. This river, unknown to them, was many miles from the Umpqua; they were on the south fork of the Coquille. As they worked their way down the Coquille, they crossed several ridges to avoid its twisting course. They found the bottom lands heavily forested with aromatic myrtles, big-leaf maples, alder, and tangles of wild cucumber vines. To their great discomfort, the travelers found the hillsides abundantly blanketed with poison oak.[33]

Determined to go north to the Umpqua, they left the river and started into the mountains, only to come to the middle fork of the Coquille. Crossing another ridge, they came to the north fork of that fingerlike stream. Traveling now without horses, exhausted and starving, the men were ready to give up when they noticed a tidal current in the river. Shortly afterward, three or four canoes manned by Indians came around a bend. These Indians pulled up on the beach near the explorers and offered to take the men downstream. T'Vault could scarcely refuse this generous offer.

At noon on September 13 the men embarked on their

[32] *Ibid.*, 17–21.
[33] *Alta California*, Oct. 14, 1851.

voyage to the sea. They found that the Coquille, although shallow at its mouth, reached for more than thirty-five tide-water miles into the coast mountains. The explorers saw dozens of Indian villages, and hundreds of people came to the riverbanks to watch them pass. The scarcity of women and children, however, made the party constantly fearful of attack.[34]

The men camped uneventfully that evening, and on the morning of September 14—a bright, clear day—they paddled on down the river. When they saw large fish weirs built with vine-maple and alder limbs tangled across the stream, they knew that the Indians were getting ready for the salmon season. They also kept close watch on the terrain. Noting how the hills to the north flattened away and merged with the coastal sand dunes, and hearing the increasing roar of the breakers, Cyrus Hedden, one of the refugees from Battle Rock the previous July, suddenly recognized that the party was near the mouth of the Coquille.[35]

Without warning, the Indians turned the canoes toward a large village on the north bank some two miles from the mouth of the river. The men of the village rushed from their lodges, jumped into the river, pulled the canoes ashore, and grappled with the explorers for their guns. Within seconds all was chaos. T'Vault later recalled:

> I looked around, and saw upon the shore the most awful state of confusion; it appeared to be the screams of thousands, the sound of blows, the groans and shrieks of the dying. At the same time I noticed my friend Brush not far distant from me, in the water, and an Indian standing in a canoe, striking him on the head with a paddle, causing the water to become bloody around him.[36]

Eventually T'Vault and Brush shoved their canoe free and paddled as fast as they could for the south shore. In the meantime, Cyrus Hedden, Lorin Williams, and Thomas

[34] Williams, "First Settlements in Southwestern Oregon," *loc. cit.*, 21.
[35] *Ibid.*, 21–22.
[36] *Alta California*, Oct. 14, 1851.

Davenport fought their way through the Indians and ran into the pines in the sand dunes behind the village. As Williams ran—cut, bruised, an arrow lodged in his abdomen, and blood seeping into his eyes from scalp wounds—he fought off two pursuers. He had nearly escaped when his pants fell down and tripped him. An Indian raised his gun to fire at him point blank, but luckily the gun failed to discharge. Williams leaped up, grabbed the musket from the Indian, clubbed him over the head, and escaped into the forest.[37]

T'Vault and Brush, going to the south, were able to reach Port Orford in two days. A few hours after the massacre, Hedden found Williams and carried him on his back for five painful days to Coos Bay and on to the Umpqua. Not until twelve days after the attack did Davenport emerge from the forests and stagger along the shore opposite Gardiner City.[38]

On the very day of the massacre significant events occurred at Port Orford. The United States Army, acting at the prompting of Governor Gaines, had dispatched a detachment of twenty dragoons under Lieutenant August V. Kautz to establish a fort in the Rogue country. The soldiers arrived there at the same time as Dr. Anson Dart, Indian superintendent for Oregon Territory. Dart had come to persuade the Rogues to cede their lands to the government.[39]

Within two days of the arrival of these men, T'Vault reached Port Orford with his tale of massacre on the Coquille, but the troops were too few to march against the Indians. Until reinforcements arrived, they cleared land and erected log buildings for their new post, Fort Orford.[40]

[37] *Oregon Statesman*, Oct. 14, 1851.

[38] A. S. Doherty, Patrick Murphy, John P. Holland, J. P. Pepper, and Jeremiah Ryan were killed at the Coquille. Hedden took his wounded friend, Williams, to Scottsburg and cared for him for four years until the arrowhead worked its way out of Williams' body. Williams, "First Settlements in Southwestern Oregon," *loc. cit. Alta California*, Oct. 14, 1851. *Oregon Statesman*, Oct. 14, 1856. Harold A. Minter, *Umpqua Valley and Its Pioneers*, 94.

[39] *Alta California*, Sept. 18, 1851.

[40] U.S. Congress, House, *House Exec. Doc. No. 93*, 34 Cong., 1 sess., 22–23.

Dart and his party visited Indian villages along the coast and within a few weeks concluded four treaties. For their lands reaching from the Coquille to the California state boundary, Dart offered the Rogues $28,500 in clothing and food. Although the treaties were forwarded to the Senate, they were never ratified.[41]

T'Vault proved himself an intrepid pioneer. Soon after his escape from the Indians he left Port Orford and returned to Oregon City. In the October 7 issue of the *Oregon Statesman* he placed this advertisement:

The subscriber intends leaving Oregon City for Port Orford, by the overland route, on Monday, the 13th inst., and wishes to employ five good men to accompany him, for the purpose of exploring the country been [*sic*] Umpqua and Port Orford. Persons desirous of availing themselves of an opportunity to explore, or go to Port Orford, are invited to join the expedition. Information given by calling at my residence in Oregon City.[42]

One of those who called was a young man named John R. Tice. On October 12 he wrote to his parents in Indiana about the bright future of Port Orford:

Tell Fred and Lizzy they must be good and when I get to Port Orford I will send them a lump of gold. . . .

The Boys are fools living in Covington [Indiana] all their life-time and see nothing. I am going to see China if I live and have luck.[43]

Tice did not get to China by way of Port Orford. T'Vault's expedition from the Umpqua west through the mountains was also a failure but not a disaster like the trip down the Coquille.

In October a new attempt was made to open a road be-

41 U.S. Congress, Senate, *Senate Exec. Doc. No. 4*, 33 Cong., special sess., 483.

42 *Oregon Statesman*, Oct. 17, 1851.

43 J. F. Santee (ed.), "Letters of John R. Tice," *Oregon Historical Quarterly*, Vol. XXXVII (1936), 26–27.

tween Port Orford and the interior. General Ethan Allen Hitchcock, commander of the Department of the Pacific, reinforced the troops at Fort Orford. He planned two expeditions: one was to punish the Coquilles for their attack on T'Vault's party; the other was to survey a route through the mountains. On October 18, 130 men, 50 of them cavalry, sailed from the division depot at San Francisco. Their 87 horses and mules and supplies cost $6,480 passage, while the rate for the men and 7 officers was $5,005. Just getting the expedition to Port Orford thus cost $11,485.[44]

The steamer *Columbia* arrived in the harbor on October 22 and, as no docks had been built, anchored a half-mile offshore. Five launches carried the supplies and the men ashore. While the crews strained with the oars and the hoists on the steamer lifted loads from the holds, the headman of a village of Indians living on the Sixes River was brought out to the *Columbia*. During a tour of the engine room, his guides put the machinery in operation "for the purpose of astonishing him and giving him an idea of the power of the peoples he was about to come in contact with." The old warrior did not seem impressed. Five days later the cavalry arrived aboard the *Sea Gull*.[45]

On October 31 parts of Company C proceeded north along the beach for the campaign against the Coquilles, while the rest of Companies A and E sailed to the mouth of the river for a beachhead landing. They found the surf churning and breaking among the rocks near the bar. These formations, well known to the Coquilles as the legendary work of Seatco, made the landing extremely dangerous. When several men nearly drowned, Lieutenant George Stoneman, later governor of California, decided to take his command back to Port Orford. A forced march on November 3 brought the two detachments together at the mouth of the Coquille.

---

[44] U.S. Congress, House, *House Exec. Doc. No. 2*, 32 Cong., 1 sess., 148–50.

[45] *Alta California*, Oct. 30, Dec. 14, 1851.

On November 5 the Indians, estimated at 150 in number, gathered along the north bank. The two groups exchanged shots, but no one was killed or wounded. That afternoon the soldiers finished building a raft, and during a cold rain Companies A and E crossed to the north side. Lieutenant Henry W. Stanton and thirty men followed along the south shore. Predictably, the Indians retreated up the river in canoes. Pursuit was almost impossible, as one of the soldiers wrote:

After four days of wading through mud and water, climbing hills, forcing passages at times through under brush almost impassable, and laying on the wet ground with only one blanket to protect us from the inclemency of the weather, we returned to the mouth of the Coquille River, having, during our march, met with nothing but deserted lodges, swamps and mountains almost impassable.[46]

Colonel Silas Casey, commander of the expedition, sent to Port Orford for three small boats. The troops embarked when they arrived but were so crowded that they found it was impossible to use their rifles. The men rowed for four days up the gently winding Coquille, noting the deserted plank lodges in clearings in the impenetrable hardwood thickets on the bottom lands. On November 20 they camped at the works of the river, near the place where T'Vault's party had begun its canoe trip. The next day Stoneman, with several men in one boat and fourteen others on the shore, proceeded up the main branch. Some eight miles from camp he found the Indians, but, when they fired at him, he ordered his force to retreat. Lieutenant Thomas Wright's detachment had an uneventful trip up the north fork toward Lee Valley.[47]

With the Indians located, the whole command turned up the main branch on November 22. Two boats, each containing five men, rowed rather contentedly up the stream.

[46] *Ibid.*, Dec. 14, 1851.
[47] *Ibid.*

When within about a half-mile of the Coquilles' camp, the men on foot divided equally to travel on either side of the river. Then, advancing silently while the boats continued their course, the troops swept toward the Indian hide-out.

The guards at the camp opened fire at the detachment in the river. Lieutenant Wright's men rushed from their hiding places and, yelling louder than the Indians, chased the enemy into the brush. Stoneman's company on the opposite shore fired into the thicket where they knew the Indians were concealed, waiting to ambush the boats. Colonel Casey shouted: "Boys, take good sight, throw no shots away, give them hell!" About fifteen Indians were killed, and two privates, French and Williams, later died of their wounds.[48]

Lieutenant Henry Stanton and the mounted dragoons of Company C did not follow the other soldiers up river on the Coquille campaign. Instead they returned to Port Orford and from there escorted Lieutenant Robert S. Williamson on two unsuccessful attempts to discover a trail to the interior. In spite of these failures, Williamson's reconnaissance resulted in one of the first maps of the region.[49]

Two other crews of a scientific nature were at work near Port Orford at this same time. An astronomical staff under George Davidson sought to fix the latitude and longitude of the harbor, and a topographical party headed by A. M. Harrison took depth readings along the coast and charted the reefs and headlands. These projects were nearing completion when the three companies of troops left Port Orford for San Francisco, where they arrived on December 12.[50]

In the meantime, Governor Gaines's treaty had not entirely quieted hostilities in the Rogue Valley. In September

[48] *Ibid.*,
[49] *Ibid.*, Dec. 1, 14, 1851. R. S. Williamson, "Sketch of the Umpqua and Rogue Rivers, & Intermediate Country," (MS).
[50] *Oregon Statesman*, Dec. 30, 1851. *Alta California*, Dec. 13, 1851. Horatio G. Gibson, *Efforts of Speech and Pen*, 23–24.

miners reported that the Indians continued to harass them while they passed along the river.[51] Positive action was immediately taken: Superintendent Dart ordered Alonzo A. Skinner, the newly appointed agent for southern Oregon, to settle in the valley. Skinner came bearing gifts and government sanction for his policies. He distributed blankets and calico to the peoples in the Umpqua Canyon, at Perkins' Ferry, and in the valley.[52]

Troubles threatened briefly in late October when the Shastas attacked four hog drovers who were driving porkers to the California mines. Each party suffered the loss of one man.[53] Skinner took the trouble lightly and remained optimistic about the Rogues' behavior. He wrote to Superintendent Dart: "From what I saw of these Indians, I am satisfied that, by the exercise of a little forebearance and discretion on the part of the whites, any further difficulties can be avoided."[54]

Failure of the miners on the Klamath to show restraint of the variety Skinner recommended brought another detachment of troops from California to the southern edge of the Rogue country that fall of 1851. Brevet Major Henry W. Wessells and several dragoons escorted Redick McKee, the new Indian commissioner for northern California. McKee, accompanied by his son John, who served as his secretary, and George Gibbs, the interpreter, left Sonoma in August.[55]

The expedition visited Indian villages in the redwood forests between San Francisco and the Klamath River. The commissioner compiled population statistics while Gibbs worked feverishly to record the languages of the people they visited. In October the party stopped at the junction of the Klamath and Trinity rivers for a conference with the popu-

---

[51] *Oregon Statesman*, Sept. 9, 1851. *Alta California*, Sept. 28, 1851.
[52] U.S. Congress, House, *House Exec. Doc. No. 1*, 32 Cong., 2 sess., 452.
[53] *Oregon Statesman*, Nov. 11, 1851.
[54] U.S. Congress, House, *House Exec. Doc. No. 1*, 32 Cong., 2 sess., 452–53.

lous bands living in that vicinity. On the sixth and the twelfth, after McKee explained that the Great Father in Washington now ruled this land, the Indians agreed to the treaties.

The impact of the miners in the region was disastrously evident. McKee found that the Indians were starving, for the tons of mining debris had muddied the creeks and rivers and had made fishing impossible. The people too were changed. Whereas they had once dressed only in finely cured deerskins and woven basket caps, they now adorned themselves with castoff garments of their white neighbors. Tragically, these people who had once been so numerous and healthy were now sickly and ridden with smallpox, measles, and tuberculosis.

The sad situation was clearly revealed to the commissioner and his party at Big Flat, a few miles up river from Happy Camp. John McKee wrote: "Two bullocks were killed, one for each rancheria, all of which was consumed by the Indians in a very short time, *entrails*, feet, and the hide, with a degree of voraciousness only equalled by hungry animals."[56] These people greatly feared the white men. Several days of patient coaxing with food and gifts were necessary to attract enough men for another council meeting.

McKee acted shrewdly, realizing that the behavior of the miners was as crucial as that of the Indians for keeping the peace. He urged prospectors in each camp to observe the agreements and to treat the Indians fairly. Further, when the bands living on the upper Klamath, the Shasta, and the Scott rivers assembled in the Scott River valley in the first week in November, McKee had the miners in Happy Camp and Shasta Butte City choose delegates to be present.

On November 4 representatives of the O-de-i-lah, I-Kar-

[55] George Gibbs, "Journal of the Expedition of Colonel Redick M'Kee, United States Indian Agent, through North-western California. Performed in the Summer and Fall, 1851," in *Information Respecting the History, Condition, and Prospects of the Indian Tribes of the United States*, Pt. III, 99–100.

[56] U.S. Congress, Senate, *Senate Exec. Doc. No. 4*, 33 Cong., special sess., 167.

uck, Kos-e-tah, and Ida-kara-wark-a-ha villages signed a treaty. McKee estimated that at least three thousand Indians were represented in these negotiations. Besides giving pledges of peace and friendship, the treaty called for establishing along the lower Scott River a reservation to which, if the treaty was ratified, the Indians were to move within two years.[57]

In mid-November, caught for some days by the torrential winter rains and muddy trails in the mountains along the Klamath, McKee wrote his impressions about the Indian situation in northern California:

> Now that I have been through the whole Indian country, I am convinced in the opinion that in almost every instance of difficulty the whites have been the agressors, and some cases have come to my knowledge of wilful, brutal, and outrageous disregard of all the claims of humanity and civilized life. Until some examples are made in the punishment of such *demons* in human shape, perfect tranquility can hardly be expected.[58]

The conflicts and clashes of 1851 wiped out a great number of Indians. The Rogues—the Athapascan, Takelman, and Shastan speakers—reacted with continued hostility to the inroads of the white men in their territory. The prospective settlers at Port Orford had been forced to repel the Quatomah band. The lower Coquille peoples had without provocation attacked and massacred part of the T'Vault party. Troubles in the Rogue Valley continued according to the old pattern, with thieving Indians and passing parties firing on one another. The troubles of June and the appearance of companies of volunteers, however, were a new attempt at retaliation against the Indians. The events on the Klamath were of a pattern that would soon become too familiar in the Rogue country—miners and Indians just could not live together peacefully. With drunk and insensitive miners, fierce

[57] *Ibid.*, 176, 220–21.
[58] *Ibid.*, 222.

and sometimes wrongfully injured Indians, only troubles could develop.

The year 1851 brought a measured increase in knowledge about southwestern Oregon. The Port Orford cedar, so important in later lumbering, had been discovered, felled, and split into shingles and lumber. Lieutenant Williamson, although failing to open a trail through the mountains, had drawn the first detailed map of the southwestern Oregon coast. Government surveys were commenced at Port Orford to fix its location and chart the harbor. T'Vault's party had explored the lower forty miles of Rogue River and had viewed the richness of the Coquille Valley. Prospectors had found traces of gold on the Applegate and in the gravel bars of the Rogue. South of the Siskiyous in northern California, George Gibbs had recorded Karok, Hupa, and Shasta vocabularies, and Redick McKee had attempted to explain the government policy to the Indians.

Perhaps of even more importance, thousands of persons learned about these discoveries and ventures. The *Alta California* in San Francisco published almost weekly reports of the activities and explorations from Port Orford. The *Oregon Statesman* received letters from the first settlers on the Umpqua and covered the events in the Rogue Valley. In 1853 the Senate document series would carry the reports of McKee's journey, and that same year Henry R. Schoolcraft would edit and publish Gibbs's diary.

So winter came to the Rogue country in 1851. Port Orford, a lonely cluster of half-finished cabins, a military post with a handful of troops, a settlement with a summer harbor and no land connections to the mining camps, stood on the coast to face the southwesterly winds and rains from the Pacific. At the mouth of the Umpqua was Umpqua City with one tent and one tin-roofed building. Upstream were Gardiner City and Scottsburg—two hamlets vying for greatness. These settlements were on a river whose entrance was considered

71

so dangerous that Hudson's Bay Company ships had avoided it for years.

The Rogue Valley, still very much the realm of the Indians, had a few isolated cabins—those of Perkins, Evans, and Skinner. Wealth perhaps existed in that region, but it was south of the Siskiyous that the miners sluiced the gravel and cut shafts into the mountains. Scattered cabins and tent cities followed the crooked Klamath to the coast. Near St. George's Reef, some twenty miles south of the Oregon-California border, was the start of another trading center, Crescent City.

4

SETTLEMENT, WARS, AND TREATIES

AT THE TURN OF THE YEAR the snows piled deeper on the slopes of Mount McLoughlin, and in the Siskiyou passes long strings of mules, loaded with supplies of flour, coffee, clothing, mining pans, shovels, and even such luxuries as tenpins for boom-town bowling alleys, plodded over the Rogue trails. These were always difficult times for the Indians. They watched their stores of dried salmon, baskets of acorns, caches of seeds, and the jerked meat, smoked months before, disappear. They spent long hours huddled in their smoky plank houses telling and retelling tales of Coyote's exploits and instructing the children about proper behavior to insure the return of the salmon and the bounty of Nature. The shamans sometimes enlivened the winter days with elaborate curing ceremonies—escapades of bluff, sleight of hand, and showmanship.

In January, 1852, James Cluggage camped near Table Rock in the Rogue Valley. He was carrying supplies from Scottsburg to Yreka. When two of his mules grazing in the nearby meadows disappeared, Cluggage trailed them toward the hills to the west. He followed a stream, later known as Jackson Creek, as it cut in muddy torrents out of the oak and chaparral and flowed onto the floor of the valley. Near where the stream left the hills, the packer found gold. The strike was so rich that Cluggage and his partner, John R. Pool, and others were later said to have averaged about one hundred ounces of dust and nuggets a day.[1]

While Cluggage and Pool were feverishly at work, the Shastas who lived in villages on Bear Creek clashed with their California cousins. James Cardwell and his partners, prospectors along the Applegate in 1851, had returned to the Rogue Valley to build a sawmill near present Ashland. They witnessed the quarreling of the Indians. Cardwell recalled that the leaders in the affray were Tipsey, notable for his long hair and heavy beard, and Sullix, aptly named for his notoriously bad temper.

The battling of the Shastas revealed the usual mode of warfare among the Indians of the Pacific Coast. The emphasis was upon a show of strength and prowess rather than upon bloody retribution. The troubles stemmed from the killing of a Klamath River Indian by some of the Oregon Shastas. When Tipsey, the leader of the people on Bear Creek, refused to give a number of horses in compensation for the man's death, more than one hundred warriors from the Klamath gathered near Cardwell's sawmill to settle their score with Tipsey's people.

For three days Cardwell and his men watched the almost mock-heroic exchange between the Shastas. The opposing sides built large fires near the selected battle site; then ten or fifteen men from one side charged across the field, jumping and yelling until they were some fifty yards from their "enemy." The side attacked immediately pursued the opposing party, forcing it to retreat in a shower of arrows. The Shastas held retribution complete when a few Indians were wounded. None was killed.[2]

While the Cardwell party was clearing and building on Bear Creek and Cluggage and Pool were mining in the far

[1] *Oregon Sentinel*, Feb. 5, 1879. Herman Francis Reinhart, *The Golden Frontier: The Recollections of Herman Francis Reinhart, 1851–1869*, 34. A. G. Walling, *History of Southern Oregon, Comprising Jackson, Josephine, Douglas, Curry, and Coos Counties*, 337–38, 359–60.

[2] Cardwell, "Emigrant Company," *loc. cit.*, 14–18.

corner of the valley, one of the first settlers in the region was in great trouble. A man named Bills, most often referred to as a fellow "of questionable repute," was brought to the Willamette Valley in irons. Alonzo A. Skinner, the southern Oregon Indian agent, had learned that Bills was living with the Indians and had encouraged the attacks in 1851. Turned over to the agent for forty blankets, Bills reportedly confessed his crime.[3]

Port Orford received additional inhabitants in May when Captain William Tichenor brought his wife and three children to the small town. They were the first white family to settle on the southwestern Oregon coast. The new year brought troubles for Fort Orford. Supplies and reinforcements were sent for the post on the steamer *Captain Lincoln,* but on January 3 inclement weather caused the ship to miss the port and be driven ashore on the broad beach just north of the entrance to Coos Bay. For three months parties from the fort journeyed between Port Orford and Camp Castaway, a temporary quarters built of canvas and salvaged stores from the ship. Finally another vessel, the *Nassau,* made the first crossing of the Coos Bay bar and anchored in the calm waters of the lower bay, where the salvaged goods were reloaded. The men and supplies reached their original destination in May. The Coos Indians did not attack the castaways but by petty thefts annoyed the men in their camp.[4]

While the rain was lashing the canvas shelters of Camp Castaway, William T'Vault continued his explorations by speculation. "It is," he wrote, "now reduced to an absolute certainty that Grave creek, which the Oregon and California road crosses, is the principal branch of the Coquille river."[5] T'Vault's belief that a good road would be opened to the coast by June was only partly realized by the forest service roads

[3] *Oregon Statesman,* Jan. 20. 1852.
[4] William Tichenor, "Among the Oregon Indians" (MS), 5. U.S. Congress, House, *House Exec. Doc. No. 1,* 32 Cong., 2 sess., 103–23.
[5] *Oregon Statesman,* Feb. 7, 1852.

of the 1930's. Grave Creek, a tributary of the Rogue, is many miles from the Coquille.

The miners on Jackson Creek, Cluggage and Pool, were not able to conceal their discoveries for long. News of their rich strike spread during the spring of 1852. Hundreds of men joined the rush to the Rogue Valley, and a new boom town, Jacksonville, grew up in the foothills on the western edge of the grass-covered plains. Peace prevailed in the region until summer; then troubles which began on the Klamath spread to the Rogue country.

On June 2 the Indians murdered Calvin Woodman on a tributary of the Scott River. The miners retaliated by attacking the Shasta villages, but believed that the culprits were from Tipsey's band on Bear Creek in Oregon. Elisha Steele, leading the volunteers, crossed the Siskiyous during the night and entered the village near the Cardwell claim the next morning. The Yreka men brought with them a prisoner, the son of the headman Sullix. They captured another Indian during the day and, after learning that the volunteers from Jacksonville were gathered there, rode to the Rogue River.[6]

A landownership controversy had developed in the lower end of the valley at the Dardanelles, the narrow place where the Rogue cuts into the mountains near present Gold Hill. The Indians had killed some cattle belonging to Dr. George Ambrose, claiming the beef as payment for the land taken from them. Ambrose insisted that he had purchased the farm from William T'Vault. The Indian agent, Skinner, thought he had settled the troubles, but when the Indian headman "Sam" decided to trade two Indian children and a horse for Ambrose's two-year-old daughter, the doctor went to Jacksonville for help.

On July 15 a number of men gathered at the Ambrose cabin and talked with the Indians. About twenty Rogues

[6] U.S. Congress, House, *House Misc. Doc. No. 47*, 35 Cong., 2 sess., 44–53.

were present, and in their discussions they referred to the troubles on the Klamath. The Indians pointedly stated that the miners were at fault and that they were killing all the Indians on the Klamath. The Rogues asserted that they foresaw similar troubles in their own valley and intended to do all possible to protect their families and rights. The white men returned to Jacksonville with this story and quickly aroused great excitement among the miners. Volunteers formed under John K. Lamerick and on July 16 marched to the Ambrose place. Learning that hostilities were imminent, Agent Skinner persuaded the volunteers to wait until he could meet with the Indians.[7]

He selected a conference site near a large gravel bar in the Rogue River below Table Rock. Although tensions were mounting, with the volunteers armed and ready for trouble and the Indians aware that shooting could begin at the slightest provocation, the opposing parties gathered peacefully on the morning of July 17. Agent Skinner had persuaded almost twenty warriors to come to where the volunteers were gathered when Elisha Steele and his forces from Yreka arrived with their two prisoners and a desire to make their long ride a successful one.

Steele, coming from California, argued belligerently with the Indian agent, insisting that he was not under Skinner's jurisdiction; he would neither stack his weapons as the Oregon volunteers had done nor give up the prisoners who had been captured in Skinner's district. Finally, hoping to proceed with the conference, the agent went to the far side of the river one last time to urge "Joe" and "Sam," the headmen of the largest valley bands, to come to the meeting. Skinner was talking with them when he saw the volunteers suddenly seizing the weapons of the Indians who had assembled.[8]

The agent rushed back across the Rogue, but as he arrived, John Galvin, one of the Yreka men, thought that

[7] U.S. Congress, House, *House Exec. Doc. No. 1*, 32 Cong., 2 sess., 455–58.

[8] *Ibid.*

the son of Sullix was escaping and fired. He shot the young man in the head at close range, instantly killing him. At the sound of the gun the other Indians ran for the river and tried to swim for the distant bank while the volunteers fired at them and the people on the opposite shore.[9]

Cardwell, one of those present, recorded that most of the Indians who had come to the meeting were killed; the *Oregon Statesman* reported twenty or more dead; Skinner thought at least four were killed. With warfare initiated, the agent retreated. He wrote to the superintendent of Indian affairs: "I could be of no further service as Indian agent, not having the least influence with the company, and not being disposed to take part in the hostilities commenced. . . . I left for home, for the purpose of preparing to defend my own house and property."[10]

Guns had been fired and blood again spilled. One of the volunteers wrote: "The Cry was extermination of all the Indians by the whites and the company began to break up into small companies to go to different Indian Rancharies to clean them out."[11] On July 18, Lamerick's men attacked a village at the mouth of Evans Creek, killing several women. Most of the Indians fled to the mountains, but on the nineteenth "Sam's" band was found hiding in the willows and thickets along the river near Table Rock. The agent established peace on July 20. Skinner reported to his superiors that the acts of the volunteers were without cause. All evidence indicated that the murders on the Klamath were committed by Indians from that region. The suspects were arrested near Klamath Lake. Once again angry miners had attacked the Rogues, who were trying to follow the treaties which had been imposed on them.[12]

[9] Cardwell, "Emigrant Company," *loc. cit.*, 26.
[10] U.S. Congress, House, *House Exec. Doc. No. 1*, 32 Cong., 2 sess., 445–58.
[11] Cardwell, "Emigrant Company," *loc. cit.*, 26.
[12] U.S. Congress, House, *House Exec. Doc. No. 1*, 32 Cong., 2 sess., 458. *Oregon Statesman*, Aug. 7, 1852.

A few days after the peace was settled, on Sunday, July 25, a public dinner was held at Table Rock to honor Captain Lamerick and his volunteers for their heroic campaign—a war in which one white man was shot in the thumb with a Minié ball. Twenty-two women and over one hundred men heard the toast of J. W. Davenport:

In behalf of those who contributed to this dinner—May your generous acts on this occasion, be honored throughout this Valley; may its emblematical influence excite the independence of our Union, and may you live to see the time when the Indians of Rogue River are extinct.[13]

One other note from this first civic meeting in the Rogue Valley survives—a song specially written and sung at the dinner by a Mr. Appler:

> *Columbia's sons' adopted daughters*
> *Shriek aloud o'er land and waters*
> *The Indians have come to quarters.*

CHORUS: *Rise, rise ye Oregon's rise,*
> *Rise, rise ye Oregon's rise,*
> *Hark, hark, hark, how the eagle cries*
> *Rise, rise, ye Oregon's rise on the Indians.*

> *Sam, he was a great warrior*
> *He was correlled between two waters.*
> *Capt. Lamrick brought him to waruers [quarters?].*

CHORUS

> *Table Rock is a pretty elevation*
> *A splendid view o'er the Indian nation*
> *The place where the chieftain took his station.*

CHORUS

> *The Indians now are in subjection*
> *Old Sammy made a bad selection*
> *His chapperel was no protection.*[14]

[13] *Oregon Statesman*, Aug. 14, 1852.
[14] *Ibid.*

Perhaps fortunately, the tune of the victory song was not preserved.

Shortly after the volunteers' celebration, the first census was made of the surviving Indians living within the Rogue Valley. Agent Skinner attempted to count all bands between the Cascades and the coast range and the Umpqua Mountains and the Siskiyous. In August he reported to the superintendent of Indian affairs that there were 406 men, 443 women, 159 boys, and 146 girls, or a total of 1,154 Indians in his district. He added, "the number of children is, I apprehend, much less than the actual number."[15]

The summer and fall of 1852 were a hazardous time for the immigrants using the Applegate Trail. The Modocs ambushed several parties near Bloody Point at Tule Lake in northern California. They also attacked the Yreka volunteers going out to meet the wagon trains. When word of the massacres reached Jacksonville, a company of twenty-two men formed under John E. Ross and on September 13 went east over the Cascades to Tule Lake. The Oregon men joined the Yreka forces led by the young Indian killer, Ben Wright. They buried the bodies of the slain immigrants and for two months patrolled the area.[16]

By October most of Wright's men had returned to Yreka. The remaining forces stayed near the trail, hoping to attack the Modocs. In November, however, after having received additional supplies, they invited the Indians to a feast. Only a few Modocs came; rumors of poison circulated. Later in the month Wright and his men attacked a village whose people were preparing for winter. Reportedly only five of the forty-six Indians survived. The jubilant volunteers mutilated the bodies of their victims and paraded into Yreka with the

---

[15] U.S. Congress, House, *House Exec. Doc. No. 1*, 32 Cong., 2 sess., 453.
[16] U.S. Congress, House, *House Misc. Doc. No. 47*, 35 Cong., 2 sess., 14–16. Keith A. Murray, *The Modocs and Their War*, 24–27. John E. Ross, "Narrative of an Indian Fighter" (MS), 25–26.

scalps they had taken. The miners in the town staged a seven-day binge in celebration.[17]

Peace existed in the Rogue country throughout the fall and into the winter of 1852. Miners wandered into the hills, panned the sands of Applegate River, ventured along the streams running into the Illinois River, pushed up the Rogue, and mined the gravel bars in the ravines of the coast mountains. In December a number of men were working near the mouth of Galice Creek deep in the range where the Rogue cuts through the hills toward the ocean. For many days nothing was heard from them; then a few bodies were found. The miners in the valley believed that the Indians of "Taylor's" band on Grave Creek had murdered the prospectors. When questioned about the missing men, the Indians said that they had drowned—and perhaps they had, for the Rogue can rise rapidly in a December freshet.[18]

The winter of 1852–53 was a harsh one for both the Indians and the white men. A heavy storm hit the valley; then a silver thaw—freezing rain and arctic wind—paralyzed the region for eighteen days. Pack trains were unable to bring in supplies. One of the miners later recalled:

At Jacksonville flour got so scarce that it sold, the winter of 1852, for one dollar or a dollar and a half per pound. Salt, none to be had. . . .
The Hotell at Jacksonville sold meals for $1.50 to $2 per meal and kept a doorkeeper at the dining room to collect in advance as they went in to eat, and those who had no money were clubbed away from the door.[19]

As the spring days warmed the land, the farmers began to clear brush, cut the oaks, and plow the meadows in the Rogue country. They destroyed the sources of grass seeds,

[17] Murray, *The Modocs and Their War*, 27.
[18] Those missing included William Grendage, Peter Hunter, William Allen, and James Bacon. U.S. Congress, Senate, *Senate Misc. Doc. No. 59*, 36 Cong., 1 sess., 4, 12. *Ashland Tidings*, Sept. 13, 1878.
[19] Reinhart, *The Golden Frontier*, 58.

acorns, and camas for the Indians, and the mining population depleted the deer and the elk. Debris from sluices and rockers clouded the clear deep holes where the steelhead and rainbow trout lived. Other changes occurred. A government appropriation became known in Oregon in May. Congress approved a $20,000 grant for the survey and construction of a military road from the mouth of the Umpqua Canyon at Myrtle Creek to Camp Stewart on Bear Creek.[20] On June 6 the first election was held in Jackson County. The next week a dedication ball in Jacksonville attracted settlers from throughout southern Oregon. One enthusiastic pioneer woman, thrilled at the social gathering, proclaimed: "O! what an assemblage of beauty and soft nothings."[21]

The summer of 1853 brought fevers and the familiar pioneer malady, the ague, to the settlers and miners. Dozens were sick. Remedies like Perry Davis' Pain Killer, poultices of bread and milk, and liberal doses of whisky were prescribed for those who were ill. Summer also brought the drying winds that changed the lush greenness of the hills and the valley to brown. A tan haze collected on the horizon and hid the distant mountains. The streams trickled away, and mining became as impossible as in the snow and winter freshets. When the mining ceased, the miners turned to other pastimes—the Indians.

In mid-June some men living near the mouth of the Applegate became suspicious about the gold dust the Grave Creek Indians were spending. They concluded that "Taylor's" band had killed the seven men missing on Galice Creek the previous winter. Taking matters into their own hands, they seized "Taylor" and several other warriors. They put "Taylor" on a white horse, gave him a pipe to smoke, and dropped a noose around his neck. Before the old man could

[20] U.S. Congress, House, *House Exec. Doc. No. 1*, 33 Cong., 1 sess., 67–68.
[21] America R. Butler, "Mrs. Butler's 1853 Diary of Rogue River Valley," ed. by Oscar O. Winther and Rose Dodge Galey, *Oregon Historical Quarterly*, Vol. XLI, No. 4 (1940), 346.

ILLUSTRATIONS

Ellen, a Tolowa, making baskets at Crescent City, California, about 1920. Although dressed in "civilized" clothing, old Ellen wears a basket cap and a dentalia necklace. (Office of Anthropology, Smithsonian Institution)

"Old Doctor," a Tolowa, at Crescent City, California. This photograph was made before 1874. (Office of Anthropology, Smithsonian Institution)

Ol-ha-the or George Harney, a Tututni who survived the Rogue River wars of his childhood to become in the 1870's chief of the confederated tribes on the Siletz Reservation (Office of Anthropology, Smithsonian Institution)

Delia (opposite), a Tolowa woman, dressed in shell and bead garments in 1901 (Office of Anthropology, Smithsonian Institution)

Charley (above), a Tolowa, at the entrance to his sweathouse at Cushion Creek, California, about 1920 (Office of Anthropology, Smithsonian Institution)

90

Umpqua Mountains on September 22, 1841, as sketched by Henry
Eld of the Emmons expedition (Yale University Library)

First portrait of an Indian in southwest Oregon, made on September 21, 1841, by Henry Eld on the south fork of the Umpqua River (Yale University Library)

Massacre Camp, a frequent trouble spot on the Oregon–California trail, sketched at the Rogue River on September 27, 1841, by Henry Eld (Yale University Library)

The 1851 fight on Battle Rock as sketched five years after the battle (*Harper's Maga zine*, October, 1856)

Battle Rock at Port Orford

General Joseph Lane, Oregon territorial governor and commander of volunteers (University of Oregon)

William G. T'Vault, leader of the ill-fated 1851 explorations for a
road from Port Orford to the Rogue Valley (University of Oregon)

Table Rock and the Rogue River near Fort Lane, in a Peter Britt photograph (University of Oregon)

Captain William Tichenor, master
of the *Sea Gull* and founder of
Port Orford (Coos-Curry Pioneer
Museum, North Bend, Oregon)

Benjamin Wright, Indian agent in southwest Oregon (National Park Service)

August Valentine Kautz, commander and road explorer at Fort Orford (Brady Collection, National Archives, Washington, D.C.)

Silas Casey, commander of the expedition to the Coquille River in November, 1851 (Brady Collection, National Archives, Washington, D.C.)

Black-sand mining at Whiskey Run north of the Coquille River
(*Harper's Magazine*, October, 1856)

Early pencil sketch of Fort Jones, California (Siskiyou County Historical Society)

Jacksonville in 1856, from a painting by Peter Britt (Oregon Historical Society)

Yreka, California, in 1856 (Siskiyou County Historical Society)

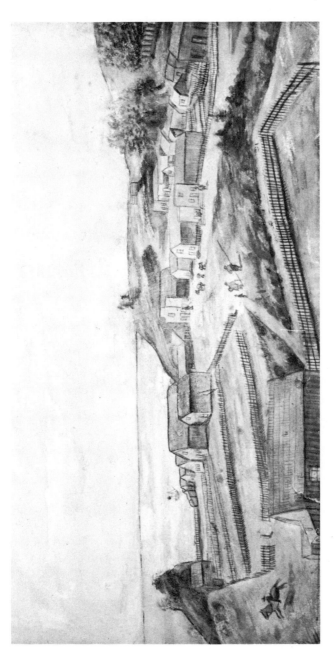

Unsigned watercolor of Port Orford, dated 1859, showing Battle Rock, the harbor, and the citizens' stockade on the hillside (Coos-Curry Pioneer Museum, North Bend, Oregon)

Chetco Indians in 1856 (*Harper's Magazine*, October, 1856)

Spear fishing for salmon by torchlight on the Oregon coast in 1856 (*Harper's Magazine*, October, 1856)

Volunteers on the march in the Rogue country (Glisan, *A Journal of Army Life*)

Edward O. C. Ord, a lieutenant during the coast campaigns of 1856 (Brady Collection, National Archives, Washington, D.C.)

General John Wool, commander of the Department of the Pacific
(Brady Collection, National Archives, Washington, D.C.)

Map of the battle at Big Meadows, the Big Bend of the Rogue River, as sketched in 1856 by Captain Thomas J. Cram (National Archives, Washington, D.C.)

114

protest, one of the men struck the horse with a board and "Taylor" was dead.[22]

The miners bound the hands of the other men behind their backs and told them to run. As the helpless Indians stumbled across the meadow the white men opened fire. A correspondent of the *Oregon Statesman* reported that another four Indians were hanged on June 17 and 18 and that "Captain" Bates and forty volunteers were rounding up the survivors. The letter writer concluded: "The Grave Creek Indians must die."[23]

By early August full summer prevailed in the Rogue country. Then, when hundreds of miners were unemployed, the Indians increased their petty thefts and, in retaliation for past injustices, murdered isolated settlers, miners, and lone travelers. The events leading to the war of 1853 probably began with the death of a man named Edwards who was living on Bear Creek near Phoenix. About August 3 friends found his body, mutilated with ax wounds. On the fourth the Rogues robbed cabins, stole some cattle, and wounded two men. They also murdered Rhodes Noland, a miner, at his cabin on Jackson Creek.[24] Fear swept Jacksonville on August 5 when an ambush occurred at the edge of town at dusk. The Indians attacked Thomas Wills, a partner in the packing company of Wills & Kyle. Several in the settlement heard Wills's screams when he was wounded; he died on August 17.[25]

The reaction to the crimes of the Indians was not long in coming. On August 6 the miners in Jacksonville hanged two Shasta Indians. Benjamin F. Dowell, who was then a packer but later a respected lawyer, wrote that late in the afternoon some settlers who had fled their homes on Butte Creek in the

---

[22] Daniel Ream, "Autobiographical Dictation" (MS), 15.

[23] *Oregon Statesman*, June 28, 1853.

[24] *Ibid.*, Aug. 30, 1853. B. F. Dowell, "Dowell's Biographies" (MS).

[25] Dowell, "Dowell's Biographies," *loc. cit.* U.S. Congress, Senate, *Senate Misc. Doc. No. 59*, 36 Cong., 1 sess., 5. Butler, "Mrs. Butler's 1853 Diary," *loc. cit.*, 352.

115

upper part of the valley arrived in town with an Indian boy
about seven years old. Upon seeing him, the miners ran
through the streets shouting, "hang him hang him. . . . Exterminate! the whole Indian race. When he is old he will
kill you."[26]

Dowell pleaded with the mob, which he estimated at
eight hundred men. His pleas for the youth were successful
until Martin Angel rode into town screaming at the top of
his voice, "exterminate the whole race. Knits [*sic*] breed lice.
We have been killing Indians in the valley all day." Within
minutes the mob had the boy hanging beside the two Shasta
men.[27]

Some of the people living in the Rogue country had been
warned that trouble was coming. Daniel Giles, a youth of
seventeen, was clerking at a small store on the Applegate
River. During the summer of 1853 he had befriended the
son and daughter of old "John," the headman of the Applegate bands. These two young people, about Giles's age, had
brought him food when he was sick with the fever, and
"John's" daughter had warned him in mid-July that her
people were restive. On August 6, when Giles was riding his
mule through the mountains to Jacksonville, he was suddenly
surrounded by the Indians. He might have been another
victim had not "John's" son "Charley," as Giles called him,
kept the Indians from killing the storekeeper. Giles found
Jacksonville in an uproar, with the volunteers organizing
and Indians hanging from the oak trees along the streets.[28]

The miners not only hanged the Indians they could find
in Jacksonville, but on August 6 decided to attack the Shasta
village on Bear Creek. These men, intent on avenging the
death of Edwards, found the Indians camped about five miles
upstream from Ashland. They rode into the village cursing

26 Dowell, "Dowell's Biographies," *loc. cit.*
27 *Ibid.*
28 Daniel Giles, "Autobiography of Daniel Giles" (MS), 16.

and shooting and felled half a dozen people in the onslaught. They took several prisoners to Jacksonville.[29]

While the volunteers were searching through the valley for Indians, a messenger carried a petition from Jacksonville to the nearest military post, Fort Jones, California. The commander at the fort, Lieutenant Bradford R. Alden, had only twenty-one men on duty, and eleven of these were sick. Nevertheless, he left immediately for the Rogue Valley with ten troopers, twenty-five muskets, five carbines, and six hundred rounds of ammunition. Passing through Yreka, he enlisted eighty volunteers. The California expedition arrived in Jacksonville on August 9.[30]

The men made their headquarters at Camp Stewart, the site used by Kearny in 1851. On August 11, Alden mustered into service an additional two companies.[31] That day, while the volunteers were fixing their camp on Bear Creek, the Rogues attacked five men at Willow Springs in the lower part of the valley. William G. T'Vault, explorer and survivor of the 1851 massacre on the Coquille, again escaped, but William R. Rose and John P. Hardin (or Harding) were killed. As dusk crept over the valley, the volunteers at Camp Stewart could see burning cabins and hay ricks in the distance. Several of Alden's volunteers deserted during the night to hurry to the defense of their own homes.[32]

Many of the miners living in the hills at the base of the Siskiyous did not come to Camp Stewart to be officially mus-

---

[29] Patrick Dunn and Andrew B. Carter of the volunteers were wounded. *Ashland Tidings*, Sept. 20, 1878. Butler, "Mrs. Butler's 1853 Diary," *loc. cit.*, 351.

[30] U.S. Congress, House, *House Exec. Doc. No. 1*, 33 Cong., 1 sess., 41–43.

[31] The volunteer commanders in 1853 were Jacob Rhodes, James P. Goodall, John K. Lamerick, John S. Miller, Robert L. Williams, and Elias A. Owens. *Ibid. Ashland Tidings*, Sept. 13, 1878. William M. Colvig, "Indian Wars of Southern Oregon," *Oregon Historical Quarterly*, Vol. IV, No. 3 (1903), 232–33.

[32] Butler, "Mrs. Butler's 1853 Diary," *loc. cit.*, 352. *Ashland Tidings*, Oct. 4, 1878. U.S. Congress, House, *House Exec. Doc. No. 1*, 33 Cong., 1 sess., 41–43.

tered into duty. Burril Griffen led a company of these "volunteers" in several forays on the Applegate. About August 10 they routed a camp of Indians near the mouth of Sterling Creek; on August 12 they were, in turn, ambushed on Williams Creek.[33]

The miners on the Applegate were reluctant to leave their claims. Some of them gathered at the small store and trading post of Holdman and Giles; others collected at a cabin about a mile up the river. The harried miners fortified their positions. The seventy-odd refugees dug trenches and maintained around-the-clock guards. Their anxieties were justified, for the Rogues attacked the cabin, killing three men and wounding several others. A few days later, when the men decided to flee to Jacksonville, the Indians ambushed them in the hills and killed another of their party.[34]

While these hostilities were taking place along the Applegate, the volunteers at Camp Stewart decided to try to trap the Indians along the river between Table Rock and the mouth of Evans Creek. On August 16 three companies under Lamerick, Goodall, and Miller left headquarters for the campaign. At first they had little success in locating their enemy, but ultimately a detachment of twenty-two men discovered some Indians (probably of "Sam's" band) on Evans Creek, some twelve miles from their usual home. Two expressmen were sent to Camp Stewart to request reinforcements.

That night, the seventeenth, the remaining volunteers camped in a meadow along Evans Creek. The field, surrounded by thickets of willows and brush, had eroded into small gullies sloping toward the stream. The Indians took advantage of the natural concealment and ambushed the camp, killing two men before the volunteers could retreat to a nearby pine-covered ridge. "Sam's" warriors, fighting

[33] In this latter battle the Indians wounded Griffen and killed Frank Garnett. *Oregon Statesman*, Aug. 23, 1853. *Ashland Tidings*, Sept. 20, 1878. U.S. Congress, Senate, *Senate Misc. Doc. No. 59*, 36 Cong., 1 sess., 13–14. *Alta California*, Aug. 21, 1853.

[34] Ream, "Autobiographical Dictation," *loc cit.*, 18.

118

for over three hours, had nearly flanked the volunteers when the Yreka companies arrived. The Indians retreated, having captured a rich prize—eighteen horses and mules loaded with blankets, guns, and ammunition.[35]

August 17 was an equally bad day for the settlers in the valley. The Rogues killed John Gibbs, William Hudgins, and three others. The farmers on Bear Creek who had fled to the cabins of Dunn and Alberding on August 13 were also attacked. Fifteen immigrants who were entering Oregon on the Applegate Trail had joined the refugees. When the Indians opened fire, many of the people were sleeping in the wagons or on the ground near the cabins. The Rogues wounded five and killed Hugh Smith, one of the immigrants.[36]

News of the widespread hostilities was quickly carried north. When Joseph Lane, the hero of the 1850 and 1851 troubles in the valley, learned of the warfare, he again hurried to the region and on August 21 arrived at Camp Stewart. Young Lieutenant Alden immediately placed his ten regulars and the several companies of volunteers under the experienced command of General Lane. The new commander divided the forces into two battalions and left headquarters on the afternoon of August 22.

Colonel John E. Ross, the leader of the volunteers against the Modocs in 1852, took one battalion down the river and then turned up Evans Creek into the mountains. Ross was commanding Miller's and Lamerick's companies. Rhodes's and Goodall's men, led by Lieutenant Alden and General Lane, went up the Rogue near Table Rock, where they found the trail of the retreating Indians.

The two battalions reunited in the rugged, brush-covered mountains north of Table Rock. The pursuit of the Rogues continued on August 23, but the chaparral and rocks made progress painfully slow and nearly impossible for the mounted

[35] The Indians killed Isham P. Keith, Frank Perry, Alfred Douglas, Asa C. Colborn, L. Stocking, and William Neff. They wounded Simeon Ely, James Carrol, John Alban, and Zebulon Shutz. *Oregon Statesman*, Sept. 7, 1853.

[36] *Ashland Tidings*, Sept. 20, 1878.

119

soldiers. The Indians further hindered the volunteers by felling trees across the trail and setting fires in the hills. A pall of smoke clouded the sky, burned the lungs of the men, and cut the visibility.

Nevertheless, near midday, the volunteers came on a recently abandoned camp where the Indians had feasted on a horse and a mule. In the late afternoon they located another camp on the main fork of Evans Creek, but as darkness swept into the hills, they lost the trail. The men camped that night in a brushy ravine without forage for their animals or adequate protection in case of attack. Throughout the night they heard the falling snags in the forest burning about them.

They found the trail of the retreating Indians again at daybreak, but a crew had to cut a path through the thick brush before the mounted forces could advance. Some distance back in the mountains, the trail left the creek and ascended a high ridge into an area untouched by the forest fires. Near midmorning the troops heard voices and shots in the distance. The Indians, encamped at a spring on the side of a mountain, were unaware that their pursuers were closing in on them.

Lieutenant Alden, taking most of Goodall's company, proceeded directly along the trail for the camp. Rhodes's men swept into a flanking movement down a ridge to the left of the trail, but not finding a suitable firing position, they joined Alden's attacking force. The Indians, caught by surprise, were fired upon when the volunteers were about thirty yards from the campsite. The yells of the white men, the war cries of the Rogues, the howling of the Indian dogs, and the smell of powder filled the morning air.

In the first attack Captain Pleasant Armstrong was killed and Lieutenant Alden was wounded. General Lane had not accompanied the forward assault, but when most of the rear guard arrived at the ridge, he led these men forward through the timber to where he found the wounded lieutenant being held by one of his sergeants. Here Lane learned that the

Indians had good protection in their camp from the fallen trees and logs and decided that only a direct onslaught would drive them from their position. Lane led the charge but, when about thirty yards from the Indians, was felled by a Minié ball in his right shoulder. The former general, directing his men to hide behind trees, continued to give orders for nearly three hours until he was so weakened by loss of blood that he was removed to the rear lines.

Within another hour the Indians cried out that they wanted peace; the interpreters confirmed their requests. Although severely wounded, Lane went to meet the Rogues. He conferred with "Joe," "Sam," and "Jim," the headmen whose people had so stubbornly resisted the soldiers. They told Lane that they were sick of war and would come to Table Rock for treaty talks within seven days. They agreed to surrender their weapons and, if necessary, submit to the "protection" of Lane's forces.[37]

The soldiers remained near the battle site another two days. They buried their dead on the ridge in the mountains. Eight Indians were killed in the battle; twenty were wounded and seven of these later died, probably from lack of any medical attention. "The Indians," wrote one of the soldiers, "as soon as the firing ceased, carried out water to our wounded men, and furnished a party to assist in conveying the litters with our wounded for 25 miles, through the mountains. This appears to be a new feature in Indian warfare."[38]

While the tired volunteers worked their way out of the hills from the headwaters of Evans Creek, Owens' company continued the search for hostile Indians farther down the Rogue. They lured several of the Grave Creek band, people who had for years harassed passing travelers on the trail, to the cabin of "Captain" Bates, offering roasted beef and friend-

[37] U.S. Congress, House, *House Exec. Doc. No. 1*, 33 Cong., 1 sess., 37–41. *Oregon Statesman*, Sept. 6, 1853.

[38] The volunteers lost Armstrong, John Scarborough, Isaac Bradly, and Charles Abbe, or Abbot. *Oregon Statesman*, Sept. 6, 1853. *Alta California*, Sept. 19, 1853.

ship. When the Indians appeared, the white men murdered five or six.[39] Those who escaped this double-dealing pillaged and burned the cabins along Jump Off Joe Creek and on August 28 ambushed Owens' volunteers at Long's Ferry near Grants Pass.[40]

Up river the companies of volunteers and the Indians began assembling at Camp Alden, a site near Table Rock that later became Fort Lane. The victorious volunteers were a disgusting sight to some of the settlers in the valley. America Rollins Butler noted in her diary that they "get drunk sware fight and disgrace themselves as rashional beings."[41] Reinforcements continued to pour into the valley but were too late to assist in the warfare. Captain Andrew J. Smith and his dragoons from Fort Orford had journeyed through the mountains to Camp Alden; Lieutenant August V. Kautz and James Nesmith arrived from Fort Vancouver on the Columbia with additional ammunition and a twelve-pound howitzer.[42]

Near midafternoon on September 1 the soldiers and Indians gathered at Camp Alden for a military parade. The guard of honor was the recently arrived company of volunteers from the coast, the Crescent City Guard. These men, so recalled B. F. Dowell, had marched through Jacksonville earlier in the day, "waving a flag on which was inscribed in flaming colors *Extermination*."[43] Several volunteer commanders made speeches. General Lane presented two banners, gifts of the ladies of Yreka, to the companies from Siskiyou County. When the soldiers finished parading, "Joe," the powerful old chief of the Takelmas, was allowed to speak. He stated that his band did not begin the hostilities. He blamed the Shastas.

39 *Oregon Statesman*, Sept. 20, 27, 1853. *Alta California*, Sept. 19, 1853.

40 They killed James Mango, Thomas Parnell, and Thomas Frizell. *Oregon Statesman*, Sept. 27, 1853. *Ashland Tidings*, Oct. 4, 1878, *Alta California*, Sept. 11, 1853.

41 Butler, "Mrs. Butler's 1853 Diary," *loc. cit.*, 354.

42 U. S. Congress, House, *House Exec. Doc. No. 1, 33* Cong., 1 sess., 37–41.

43 MS P–A 133.

"Joe" asserted that he led his men to war only when the whites had killed fourteen of his people, many of whom were servants in Jacksonville.[44]

On September 4 treaty negotiations opened on a narrow bench of land near the foot of Table Rock on the north side of Rogue River. Lane, his arm in a sling, was wearing fatigue dress; "Joe," described as "tall, grave, and self possessing," wore a long black robe over his regular clothing. The chief's daughter, "Mary," stood at his side. In the conference circle were Captain Andrew J. Smith from Fort Orford, Captain Benjamin Alvord and Jesse Applegate of the party surveying the military road, the volunteer commanders, and Judge Matthew Paul Deady, who was on his way to Jacksonville to open the first district court in southern Oregon. While the men in "Joe's" band, armed with bows and arrows, gathered on the distant hillsides, the dragoons from Fort Orford formed at the base of Table Rock in case armed intervention should be necessary. Discussion progressed slowly as the interpreters explained the deliberations.[45]

On September 8 an agreement was concluded with the Indians under the leadership of the two brothers, "Joe" (Aps-er-ka-har) and "Sam" (To-qua-he-ar), and the sub-chief, "Jim" (Ana-chah-a-rah). The principal features of the treaty were cession of Indian land titles and the establishment of a reservation. The Rogues agreed to exchange guns, except for a few for the headmen, for clothing and blankets. The white men demanded that when the Indians were eventually paid for their ceded lands—most of the Rogue Valley—up to $15,000 was to be used to pay the damage claims of settlers in the region.[46]

Open warfare nearly flared again on September 9 when the Indians learned that Williams' company had captured

[44] *Oregon Statesman*, Sept. 27, 1853. *Alta California*, Sept. 19, 1853.

[45] Matthew Paul Deady, "Letters, Dictations, and Related Biographical Material, 1874–1889" (MS), *Oregon Statesman*, Sept. 27, 1853.

[46] Kappler (ed.), *Indian Affairs*, 1050.

and executed one of the last men in "Taylor's" band from Grave Creek. They had tied the man to a tree and had shot him.[47] The agreement of September 8 was never ratified by the Senate, but a similar treaty of September 10, signed by five additional headmen, was approved. The reservation was specifically delineated as extending up Evans Creek to a small prairie, across the mountains to Upper Table Rock, south to Rogue River, and down the river to the mouth of Evans Creek. Lane set $60,000 as the cession price for all the lands in the valley. The government promised to build houses on the reservation for the principal headmen. The treaty was signed by Joel Palmer, superintendent of Indian affairs for Oregon; Samuel H. Culver, the new Indian agent in the valley; and eight headmen representing 287 Indians.[48]

For the third time General Lane had successfully obtained promises of peace from the Indians of the Rogue country. Lane was a rough-and-tumble politician and pioneer. A graphic picture of him was written while he was at the headquarters at Camp Alden, a log cabin with only a smoke hole in the ceiling. A man who went to see Lane wrote:

But fancy my surprise on being introduced to a robust good looking middle aged man, with his right arm in a sling, the shirt sleeves slit open and dangling bloody from his shoulder, his nether extremities cased in an old pair of gray breeches that looked as though they were the identical ones worn by Gen. Scott when he was "exposed to the fire in the rear." One end of them was supported by a buck skin strap in the place of a suspender, while one of the legs rested upon the toe of the remains of an old boot. His hair so twisted, tangled and matted that it would have frightened the teeth out of a curry comb, and set all tonsorial operations at defiance, was surmounted by the remains of an old forage cap, which, judging from its appearance, might have been worn at Braddock's defeat. This composed the uniform of the old hero who never surrendered.[49]

[47] *Oregon Statesman* (Sept. 27, 1853). *Alta California* (Sept. 24, 1853).
[48] Kappler, (ed.), *Indian Affairs*, 603–605. *Annual Report of the Commissioner of Indian Affairs, 1854*, 294.
[49] *Oregon Statesman*, Sept. 27, 1853.

Two surviving accounts, one by the Indians and another by one of the settlers in the valley, give some of the details about the causes of the war in 1853. While Lane was at Camp Alden near the treaty grounds, he held "Ben" and "Mary," the children of the headman "Joe," as hostages. "Mary," talking with Lane in Chinook jargon, told him that shortly before the hostilities commenced, an Indian named Pe-ous-i-cut, a Shasta in Tipsey's band from Bear Creek, had sold an Indian woman to a card dealer in Jacksonville.

When the man refused to pay, a fight ensued, the miners siding with the card dealer. Pe-ous-i-cut returned to Tipsey's camp, where the Shastas were trading skins and horses with "Joe's" people. Pe-ous-i-cut persuaded the Shastas to attack the white men. "Joe's" men did not know about the actual hostilities until Tipsey's men came to their camp and said that the white men were killing all the Indians and that they must unite and fight for their homes. Old "Joe," according to his daughter's story, wanted to go to Jacksonville to learn whether the men from Tipsey's band were telling the truth, but the presence of armed white men, the urging of Tipsey, and the wishes of his own young men persuaded "Joe" to lead his people into the hills to the place where the battle occurred on August 24.[50]

A story closely paralleling "Mary's" was given in the autobiography of Benjamin F. Dowell of Jacksonville. He was perhaps correct when he wrote: "In 1853 the Rogue River War was caused by bad whites and vindictive Indians." Dowell explained that in July, Edwards, the first man murdered, stole a Shasta slave from "John's" band and refused to pay the owner. The men in "John's" band, who lived on the Applegate, decided to fight the whites. A number of Shastas who had been driven over the mountains by the miners on the Klamath assisted them in their warfare. On August 3 or 4 they murdered Edwards and initiated the war.[51]

[50] Lane, "Autobiography," *loc. cit.*, 117–25.
[51] Dowell, MS, P-A 133, pp. 3–4.

Tipsey's band, the one probably most involved in the hostilities, did not attend the treaty discussions at Table Rock. A few nights after the Indian girl told Lane her version of the troubles, she told him that Tipsey's people were hiding on the distant slopes of the Siskiyous. Lane, carrying his arm in a sling, and Robert B. Metcalf, the interpreter, left the next morning to find these people.

Lane purchased a few presents for the Indians in Jacksonville and then searched all day with Metcalf in the brush and ravines of the Siskiyous. Sometime after dark, while wandering through the trees and boulders along the Applegate, the two men stumbled into the Shastas' camp. For a few moments both sides were ready to open fire, but, at length, Metcalf explained that he and Lane had come in peace. Two days later Tipsey signed an agreement, but it was never ratified. Lane distributed clothing to those men agreeing to the document. Pe-ous-i-cut was absent, but instructions were left that he would be given his gift when he came to Jacksonville to sign. When Pe-ous-i-cut arrived there, the miners arrested him. They summarily tried, convicted, and hanged him.[52]

Peace returned to the Rogue, but troubles flared in the distant hills and meadows along the Illinois River where miners were working the rich diggings on Althouse and Sucker creeks. On the night of September 12 the Indians attacked several prospectors at the placer bars in the Illinois. A company of volunteers from the region, commanded by Robert Williams, fared badly the same day. They battled Indians on the Applegate until sunset and, although they wounded a dozen of the enemy, were unable to compel the Indians to surrender.[53]

When news of these troubles reached Camp Alden, Captain Smith sent a troop detachment to the Illinois Valley. These men found too much cattle-thieving and hostility and

[52] Lane, "Autobiography," *loc. cit.*, 125–27.
[53] Thomas Phillips was killed in the hostilities on the Applegate. *Alta California*, Sept. 24, 1853. *Ashland Tidings*, Feb. 29, 1879.

waited for reinforcements, which arrived on September 22, before pursuing the Indians to their camp in the Siskiyous. The troops and their guides attacked immediately on sighting the village and possibly killed fifteen people. They captured sixteen horses and burned all the baskets, stores of food, skins, and other Indian property which they could find. The Indians wounded two soldiers in the encounter and later in the day downed four more in an ambush. The soldiers believed that the Indians were strangers in the area. Perhaps they were, for many of the Tolowas had fled the coast when volunteers attacked their villages at Lake Earl and on the Smith River.[54]

Again troubles in the interior of the Rogue country had shown the need for permanent military assistance. Fort Jones was over the Siskiyous in California; Fort Orford was nearly one hundred miles distant through the densely forested coast range. Thus in late September, Captain Andrew J. Smith established Fort Lane about a mile below Table Rock on the south side of Rogue River. By November, Captain George Patton commanded the post. Four companies, or a total of one hundred men, were on duty.[55]

On October 7, James Kyle, a partner of Thomas Wills, one of the first men killed at the commencement of the war in August, was ambushed by two Klamath River Indians near Willow Springs. "Joe," a distant relative of these men by marriage, turned the two murderers over to the troops at Fort Lane on October 11 to show his peaceful intentions and willingness to follow the treaty.[56]

Troubles also threatened briefly on Cow Creek, a tributary of the South Umpqua River. The five bands of Athapascan speakers who lived there had decreased to about half their numbers because of an epidemic during the harsh winter of 1852–53. On September 14 approximately two hundred sur-

[54] *Oregon Statesman*, Nov. 22, 1853.
[55] *Ibid.*, Oct. 18, 1853. U. S. Congress, House, *House Exec. Doc. No. 1*, 33 Cong., 1 sess., 122–23.
[56] *Oregon Statesman*, Nov. 8, 1853.

vivors were represented in treaty agreements ceding their lands for a small reservation in the region. Then fourteen men, some of them the "exterminators" who had murdered the Indians of Grave Creek, arrived in the Cow Creek valley, killed an old man and an old woman, and left a baby to die in the burning camp. The next day, the Indians and settlers alike surrounded the murderers, who escaped only by promising that they would not return. The settlers persuaded the Umpquas to present their grievances to the Indian superintendent the next time he visited the area.[57]

The troubles of August and September had been costly not only in lives but also in dollars. The volunteers readily put forth their claims for remuneration for defending the United States:

1. For transportation, including hire of horses, mules, wagons, etc. — $18,198.00
2. For forage, consisting of oats, barley, and hay — 29,675.68
3. For ferriage — 167.50
4. For quartermaster supplies — 7,996.20
5. For subsistence in kind and meals — 32,241.57
6. For ordnance, including guns and ammunition — 1,862.97
7. For medicines and hospital purposes — 9,136.90
8. For miscellaneous projects and items not classified — 8,008.38

$107,287.20

The volunteers had consumed 29,100 candles, 19,000 bars of soap, 14,432 rounds of powder, and 10,184 pieces of lead.[58] It is doubtful that ever before or since in the early history of southwestern Oregon had the pioneers seen such bright nights, been so clean, or fired so many shots.

In addition to the supply costs, the volunteers, totaling in all 441 men, claimed 16,974 days of service for themselves and 13,882 days of service for their animals. They requested $15,390.08 for wages. (Another calculation which they submitted, supposedly based on rates recommended by Lieuten-

[57] Riddle, *Early Days in Oregon*, 47–48, 76–79.

ant Alden, requested $11,962.37 in pay for the men, and
$46,560.00 for the use of their horses and mules.)[59] War was
more profitable than gold-mining!

The troubles of 1852 and 1853 were yet more expensive
for the federal government. Many of the settlers in the valley
and along the river filed damage suits for destruction of
property under Article Three of the treaty of September 10.
Their claims as determined by a board of commissioners
totaled $43,140.[60]

The Rogue Indians had had to pay in a more sinister
accounting as war and civilization took their toll. For a decade
and a half the Indians of the upper valley were in intermittent
contact with travelers and traders passing through their lands.
The travelers came and went. When they left, the land and its
resources were still available to the Indians. The prospectors
and military campaigns of 1851 were more of a threat, but
Indian tenure survived.

Quite different were the consequences in 1852 and 1853.
Settlers and gold seekers moved in, fenced the open fields,
allowed hogs to run free and root out the camas bulbs, killed
the game, and plowed under the grass, the seeds of which had
been a prime food for the Indians.

These uninvited residents also were callous killers of
Indian men, women, and children. They attempted to force
the survivors to subsist on a hilly and rocky reservation. In
September, 1853, perhaps half the Rogues accepted the treaty
conditions and came to live under the agent's supervision.
Only the more warlike held out.

Throughout the valley, signs of the white men were now
clearly in evidence. Perhaps the changes that had occurred are
best reflected in the lines written by an immigrant who in late

[58] U. S. Congress, House, *House Exec. Doc. No. 99*, 33 Cong., 1 sess.,
2–5.

[59] *Ibid.*

[60] U. S. Congress, House, *House Exec. Doc. No. 52*, 38 Cong., 2 sess.,
2–5.

September descended the slopes of the Cascades after a six-month trip across the continent:

we beheld an inclosed field, with shocks of grain, a house surrounded by gardens, people, and appurtenances of civilization. . . . It was a picture varied with shadow and sunshine, lofty mountains and little hills, meadows, groves, and silvery streams, altogether more beautiful than a painter could portray, or even imagine.[61]

[61] John Beeson, *A Plea for the Indians: With Facts and Features of the Late War in Oregon*, 22.

BLACK SAND GOLD AND MASSACRES

THE OCEAN has been good to the people who have lived in southwestern Oregon. The Indians found in the tidal pools, among the purple and giant orange urchins, an abundance of invertebrates. Hard-working women pried and plucked the leathery but edible chitons, limpets with dome-shaped caps of shell, piddocks, barnacles, snails, and other animals of the "splash zone" from their sandstone perches and dropped them into their collecting baskets. From the ocean came the stranded whales, the annual runs of salmon, the summer spawning of smelt, the sea lions, and the richly furred otter. On the scattered rocky islands along the coast, the men defied the rough surf to raid the nests of pelicans, cormorants, and gulls. They found shattered but usable pieces of fir, alder, and cedar, and occasional redwood logs tossed onto the beaches during the storms. The sea was the great giver to the early residents of the coastal Rogue country.

The white settlers who came to that region found that the ocean was an integral part of their lives. It was their link with the outside world. Infrequent steamers, like the aptly named *Sea Gull* and *Ocean Bird*, brought letters and aging newspapers, clothing, salt, tinned goods, and other reminders of civilization. These people were ready to exploit their environment, for they knew that an otter pelt would bring seventy-five or one hundred dollars in San Francisco. Like the Indians, they collected mussels, caught the salmon, dug for clams, and scavenged for eggs and feathers.

The wealth of the Pacific did not show itself all at once to those who lived along the shores. Although it had been there for centuries, discerning eyes were needed to discover one of the richest gifts of the sea—black sand gold. The miners who came to Port Orford in 1851 had searched for gold, but their prospecting was limited by their experiences in the mines of the Sierras. They sought "coarse gold," flakes and nuggets that glittered in the bottom of their mining pans as they sloshed away the gravel, sand, and muddy water. To these miners, coastal southwestern Oregon had been a humbug; gold was there, but it was too difficult to find and too scarce to compete with the El Dorado that was California.

For more than two years after the first settlers had come to Port Orford, the winds blew and shifted the sands, the sun glistened on its fine chromium deposits, and the waves washed, buried, and redeposited it. Then in the spring or early summer of 1853, about the time the flurry of troubles erupted between the miners and the Indians in the Rogue River valley, two young half-bloods, John and Peter Groslius from French Prairie in the Willamette Valley, looked closely at the black sands north of the Coquille River and found rich traces of fine gold dust. The brothers, who as children had traveled on the 1833 Hudson's Bay Company brigade through the Rogue country, worked their claim and took the gleanings to be weighed at Scottsburg. By the time the news of their discovery had reached Yreka, it was proclaimed that they had "taken out 150 lbs. of the genuine *oro*."[1]

Undoubtedly their claim was a rich one, for the Groslius brothers soon lost it to shrewder operators, the McNamaras. As information about the beach mines spread, the men living at Port Orford almost completely abandoned the town and rushed to the newly named Randolph mines at Whiskey Run Creek. The miners brought with them the riffle-box technique, introduced at Port Orford in April, by which a profitable amount of dust could be caught in the sluicing. The rewards

[1] *Alta California*, Dec. 3, 1853.

were rich for those miners who first reached the beaches north of the Coquille. Water was still abundant for mining; the summer low tides allowed several hours of undisturbed work on the beach, and competition was scarce. Steamers had not stopped at Port Orford for almost two months, and not until July did the reports of the strike reach San Francisco.[2]

The influx of miners brought other discoveries of gold on the beaches. Men who only a few months before had rushed to the diggings on Althouse and Sucker creeks, to the mines on Jump Off Joe Creek, Galice Creek, or the Applegate, now established villages in clusters near the mouth of the Rogue. They built Elizabethtown, Logstown, and Prattsville north of the river and developed Whalesburg, later known as Ellensburg and then Gold Beach, on the south side on a narrow bottom land between the sea and the hills.

Another type of mining had further stimulated interest and settlement in southwestern Oregon in the spring of 1853. In May, Perry B. Marple, an explorer and land promoter, organized the Coos Bay Commercial Company in Jacksonville. He had explored the harbor which had been briefly settled by the castaways from the *Captain Lincoln* in 1852, and spoke of it in glowing terms. His enthusiasm captivated several men, and by October they had moved their families to Empire City, a town they hoped to develop on Coos Bay.[3]

The harbor was a good one, provided ships could find a favorable breeze and a passage across the two-mile-wide ocean bar. The bottom lands around the bay and its tributaries promised good farming. But another commodity had stimulated the migration to Empire—coal. The explorers had found rich veins, many of them reaching to the water's edge, a stone's throw from the holds of transport vessels. By October the pioneer speculators had staked out nineteen claims.[4]

Each intrusion of the white men meant changes in the

[2] *Ibid.*, July 15, 1853.
[3] Agnes Ruth Sengstacken, *Destination West!*, 110–15.
[4] *Alta California*, Oct. 1, 1852.

life of the Indians. Shanty towns sprawled over their former village sites; the settlers planted potatoes in the rich soil of the old middens and cemeteries. Whisky, firearms, life without women, and memories of Indian atrocities at Battle Rock and against the T'Vault party in 1851 stoked the potential fires of hostility between the settlers and miners and the Indians. Yet, while the feverish prospecting and mining continued through 1853, peace held along the Oregon coast.

However, just south of the territorial border, in northern California, the settlers attempted to drive the Tolowa bands from their homes. Ida Pfeiffer, who visited these people and stayed with the Chetcos in November, remarked several times in her travel account that she saw many burned and destroyed Indian plank houses. She sympathized with the Indians' retaliation against the white men who kidnaped and raped their wives and daughters. One Smith River village, Hawunkwut-was was burned in 1853, and some seventy people were murdered.[5] In January, 1854, seven more Indians were killed on Smith River. The inhabitants at the port of Crescent City formed a volunteer guard—perhaps the same one that had gone to the Rogue Valley too late to fight in the war the previous August—which marched through the redwood forests to Smith River to "protect" the settlers there.[6]

As the winter storms of 1853–54 tore at the rude plank shacks of the miners at Randolph, Port Orford, Elizabethtown, Prattsville, and Whalesburg, making work on the beaches impossible, the men, known to the more respectable pioneers as the "exterminators," began to spread their stories, retell old crimes of the Indians, and inflame fears. Several of these men, living near the ferry at the mouth of the Coquille River, called a meeting on January 27. The miners at Randolph and the cabins along the beach left their games of keno, euchre, monte, and poker to assemble that night.

[5] Pfeiffer, *A Lady's Second Journey Round the World*, 319–20. Curtis, *The Hupa, Yurok, Karok, Wiyot, Tolowa and Tututni, Shasta, Klamath*, 91–92.

[6] *Alta California*, Jan. 19, 1854.

The meeting was orderly and planned to show, at least in outward appearance, its legality. A. F. Soap presided and William H. Packwood, one of the men shipwrecked at Camp Castaway in 1852, served as secretary. The miners leveled five grievances against the Nasomah band of the lower Coquilles. They specifically complained that an Indian had ridden a horse without permission, that the ferry rope had been mysteriously cut, and that the Indians had refused to come to a conference with the self-appointed leaders of the miners.[7]

On January 28 seventy-three men attended a second meeting. They resolved that the minutes of their session be sent to the Oregon newspapers and to the Indian agent at Port Orford. Thus vying for public approval, having gone through the formality of notifying the agent, who could not possibly have arrived before they acted, the Coos County volunteers adjourned, to reassemble shortly before dawn. Early that morning, while the Indian men, women, and children were still asleep in their village houses, forty volunteers under George H. Abbot attacked this settlement. The Coquilles, roused from their lodges, had only three guns and their bows and arrows with which to fight. Their attackers singled out the men and murdered fifteen of them. They also killed one woman and wounded two others.[8]

That same evening, S. M. Smith, the Indian agent, and Lieutenant August V. Kautz from Fort Orford, after a long and fruitless trip, arrived at the Coquille. They were too late to settle any problems which may have existed; they could only write their superiors about the gun-happy miners. In one further meeting, the volunteers congratulated themselves for their actions in quelling an imminent Indian war. Very probably their murders provoked the Coquilles, who retaliated during the next few months.[9]

[7] *Annual Report of the Commissioner of Indian Affairs, 1854*, 272.

[8] *Ibid.*, 268. U. S. Congress, House, *House Exec. Doc. No. 76*, 34 Cong., 3 sess., 86–87.

[9] Dodge, *Pioneer History of Coos and Curry Counties, Oregon*, 93–94.

In February or March the Coquilles murdered two trappers, Elijah Burton and a man named Venable, near Iowa Slough. Shortly thereafter the Indians ambushed James Lowe and his partner as they were paddling up the river. The white men returned the fire and thought they killed two Indians and wounded another. A few weeks later, alerted to the troubles, the settlers at Coos Bay captured two Coquille men. They charged them with murdering Venable and Burton. The men were given miner's justice at the end of a rope thrown over the limb of a pine tree on the bluff near Randolph.[10]

Less than two weeks after the massacre of the Nasomah band on the Coquille a similar mass murder occurred at two large Indian villages near the mouth of the Chetco River. Where Jedediah Smith and his party had forded the stream at low tide in 1828, the Indians operated a small ferry for the miners and packers who passed along the coast. They took trinkets, beads, and castoff clothing for payment. They had experienced no troubles with the white men until the fall of 1853 when A. F. Miller came to the Chetco, selected a land claim about a quarter-mile from the river mouth, and built his cabin in the midst of one of the villages.

In spite of the protests of the Chetco bands, Miller decided to control the ferry business. He promised peace, and, trusting him, the Indians gave up their guns. Treacherous Miller then called in his friends from the Smith River in California and about February 15 attacked the villages. They burned two men to death when they fired the plank houses and shot another when he attempted to escape through the round entry hole at the corner of his house. The "exterminators" allowed most of the women and children to escape but murdered twelve men in all.[11]

---

[10] "Notes on Coos Bay" (MS), 38–39. Giles, "Autobiography of Daniel Giles," *loc. cit.*, 26–27.
[11] *Annual Report of the Commissioner of Indian Affairs, 1854*, 258.

These inhumane and irresponsible acts on the Coquille, the Chetco, and the Smith rivers instilled lasting hatreds and fears in the Indians. When Joel Palmer, superintendent of Indian affairs, visited these coast villages in May, most of his attempts to meet the Indians were unsuccessful. They were too afraid to confer with any white man. Largely through Palmer's insistence, Miller was arrested and brought to Fort Orford, where he was held for six weeks for his crimes. When examined by a justice of the peace, however, he was, according to the agent, "set at large on the ground of justification and want of sufficient evidence to commit."[12]

Palmer understood the tragedy that was befalling the Indians of the Rogue country. He reported that the many bands of Rogues wanted peace and were willing to allow the white people to settle in the region if only they would be left alone and allowed to retain their fisheries. Several of the headmen with whom he had been able to confer had told him that they wanted to learn about agriculture. A few bands were planting potatoes.[13] Comments similar to Palmer's were made by Herman Francis Reinhart, a young miner who opened a guesthouse on the Port Orford–Rogue River trail in May. He testified to the honesty of the Indians and recalled: "The Indians were friendly and were well pleased for us to take up land and cultivate, and never offered to molest us."[14]

In July, acting upon orders from Superintendent Palmer, Josiah Parrish, the new agent at Port Orford, submitted his survey of the bands living along the coast and for some forty miles up the Rogue River. Parrish found 1,311 Indians living in fourteen villages and possessing twelve guns. The census is particularly interesting since Parrish named each band and gave its location:[15]

[12] *Ibid.*, 258. Josiah L. Parrish, "Anecdotes of Intercourse with the Indians" (MS), 69–70.

[13] *Annual Report of the Commissioner of Indian Affairs, 1854*, 259.

[14] Reinhart, *The Golden Frontier*, 80.

[15] *Annual Report of the Commissioner of Indian Affairs, 1854*, 495.

Band	Location	Population
Nas-o-mah	Mouth of Coquille River	59
Choc-re-le-a-tan	Forks of Coquille River	105
Quah-to-mah	Sixes River, Elk River, Port Orford	143
Co-sutt-heu-tun	Mussel Creek	27
Eu-qua-chee	Euchre Creek	102
Yah-shute	Mouth of Rogue River	120
To-to-tin	Lower Rogue River	120
Mack-a-no-tin	Lobster Creek to Illinois River	124
Shis-ta-koos-tee	Forks of Illinois and Rogue to Big Bend	153
Chet-less-na-tin	Pistol River	51
Wish-te-na-tin	Whaleshead	66
Che-at-tee	Chetco River	241

Shortly after this enumeration was compiled, Parrish, a former Methodist missionary who had come to Oregon in 1840 as part of Jason Lee's reinforcement, left Port Orford, and Palmer appointed a new breed of Indian agent. The superintendent's choice was Benjamin Wright, the Indian killer from Yreka who was feared and respected by the Indians. Parrish recalled that his successor was very intemperate, for the new agent had scandalized even the miners at Port Orford when he stripped the government interpreter, Chetco Jenny, and whipped her as she ran naked through the streets of the town.[16]

The beach mines of southwestern Oregon flourished through their second season when the tides were at their extremes. Then the boom faded. As the summer of 1854 passed and the ocean surf covered the beaches for longer periods each day and the unworked sands became increasingly scarce, the people left for other diggings. Sand drifted into the whipsaw pits at Randolph, where only months before teams of men had feverishly rolled logs onto the braces, sweated and sworn at the sawdust as they cut the planks for the riffle boxes and slab houses.

One last flurry for gold occurred on the upper reaches of the south fork of the Coquille River. Thomas Johnson had

[16] Parrish, "Anecdotes of Intercourse with the Indians," *loc. cit.*, 82.

138

found nuggets in the streams far into the coast mountains. Seeing a last chance to unload their stocks of supplies, the merchants at Port Orford quickly circulated letters attesting to the richness of "Coarse Gold" Johnson's mines. But the discovery was a humbug—few men found enough gold to make the work profitable.[17]

By September, Port Orford had dwindled to a settlement of thirty-five houses, one hundred people, and twenty-five soldiers. Colonel Joseph K. F. Mansfield visited the fort on his inspection of western military posts, drew a map of the site, and wrote in his report: "I would recommend that it be abandoned as soon as it will be safe to do so."[18]

While the mining boom flourished and declined on the Oregon coast, intermittent hostilities continued in the interior of the Rogue country. The war of 1853, the treaties, the establishment of Fort Lane, and the assignment of some bands to the Table Rock Reservation had contributed much to the greater harmony of Indian-white relations in that troubled area, but there was little that well-intentioned agreements or the presence of soldiers and agents could do when the "exterminators" went to work.

When the miners were left idle by the enforced January layoff, nineteen men from Sailor's Diggings decided to attack the snowbound Indian lodges along the Illinois River. They stormed one village but found only seven women, one boy, and two girls. They shot a pregnant woman nine times and murdered the little girls. Then the men retreated to the mining camp to arouse others to help them finish the massacre. Instead, the more responsible prospectors quickly sent a message to the Indian agent in the Rogue Valley, stating: "So far the Indians have been peaceable and friendly, and we do not wish

[17] Russell C. and Ellis S. Dement, "After the Covered Wagons," *Oregon Historical Quarterly*, Vol. LXIII, No. 1, (1962), 15. Emil R. Peterson and Alfred Powers, *A Century of Coos and Curry*, 133.
[18] "Col. Mansfield's Inspection Report of the Dept. of the Pacific, 1855" (MS).

to commence hostilities again as it would seem like cold blooded murder."[19]

Other miners, with wanton motives, met their fate on Cottonwood Creek near the Klamath River in late January when the Shastas killed four "squaw hunters" who were molesting their women.[20] Although the white men had caused the trouble, the regular troops at Fort Jones were compelled to pursue the Indians to quell the disturbance. Lieutenant George Crook, the later famous frontier general and one of the officers in this expedition, sadly recalled:

It was of no unfrequent occurrence for an Indian to be shot down in cold blood, or a squaw to be raped by some brute. Such a thing as a white man being punished for outraging an Indian was unheard of. It was the fable of the wolf and the lamb every time.[21]

Crook, Henry Judah, John Bonnycastle, and some twenty soldiers from Fort Jones rode to Yreka where the volunteers joined their detachment. They found that the snow was deep and that freezing rains had iced over the brush and rocks. The poor Indians, fearing they might be pursued, had taken refuge from the stormy weather and the white men in a cave near the river. Captain Judah, commander of the "forty thieves" who were the regular troops at Fort Jones, protected himself from the cold by guzzling whisky. Many of the other soldiers did likewise, and the expedition, so Crook remembered, consisted of drunken men spread along ten miles of snowbound trail.

In spite of Judah's delirium tremens and other mishaps, the soldiers found the Shasta hide-out. Learning that the Indians were well fortified, Crook rode to Fort Lane to borrow a cannon. A company of soldiers from that post returned with the howitzer to the Klamath, and on January 26 the soldiers

[19] *Oregon Statesman*, March 7, 1854. U. S. Congress, Senate, *Senate Exec. Doc. No. 16*, 33 Cong., 2 sess., 14–15.
[20] The men were John Clark, John Hadfield, Hiram Hulin, and Wesley Mayden. *Oregon Statesman*, Feb. 7, 1854. *Ashland Tidings*, Oct. 11, 1878.
[21] *General George Crook: His Autobiography*, 16.

fired a few charges into the cave. One curious volunteer commander poked his head over the cliff to spy the damage and was promptly shot by the Indians. Near dusk the Shastas sued for peace. Some fifty men, women, and children crawled out of their dark hiding place in the mountainside.[22]

The troops were satisfied that no further hostilities would occur. The soldiers packed Judah, still ill from his overindulgence, to Yreka and took the body of the dead volunteer to Cottonwood. Crook wrote: "In the whole population of several hundred people a Bible could not be had to use in performing the burial service." The young lieutenant likened the nearby town of Yreka to a seething nest of ants:

> Miner, merchant, gambler, and all seemed busy plying their different avocations, coming and going apparently all the time, scarcely stopping for the night. Idlers were the exception. . . . Everyone carried their lives in their own hands. Scarcely a week passed by without one or more persons being killed.[23]

Others besides Crook noticed the changes that had come to northern California since the discovery of gold. In February a miner in the Scott Valley estimated that several thousand men were mining in the region, but only twenty-five warriors yet survived in the villages in the valley, and not more than forty still lived along the Klamath River near the settlements. He told how the Indians had given up all their arms to the white men to show their earnest desire for peace; then the miner concluded:

> But, I must close for the present, as I want to attend a war meeting that has been called this evening, on which occasion I expect to make a speech in favor of extermination; but, like some of my friends, I also expect to take d——ish good care not to carry it out personally.[24]

---

[22] *Ibid.*, 17–20. U. S. Congress, Senate, *Senate Exec. Doc. No. 16,* 33 Cong., 2 sess., 18–19.

[23] Crook, *General George Crook: His Autobiography,* 16,20.

[24] *Oregon Statesman,* March 21, 1854.

In April the *Oregon Statesman* carried a story copied from the *California Express*. According to the account, Colonel W. Miller of Fort Brown, a post near Shasta, California, pursued a party of Indians north to the Siskiyous. His seventy-three men fought a pitched battle and killed perhaps sixty people. Miller's force suffered five privates killed and many wounded, including four officers.[25]

Throughout the winter months Agent Culver and Captain Smith at Fort Lane endeavored to confine the Rogue River Indians to their new reservation at Table Rock. They were able to bring in some of the bands from the Applegate, but the people under the headman Tipsey, whose home was on Bear Creek and in the Siskiyous, remained uncontrolled. No sooner had Culver located many of the Indians on the reserve than an epidemic struck. The agent wrote that the "bloody flux and intermittent fever" made it impossible for him to govern the stricken people. Thus, concluding that the Rogues might survive best in their old haunts, he gave permission for many families to leave the reservation.[26]

Tipsey, a militant and untamable leader, despised his kinsmen who acceded to the treaties and wishes of the newcomers. His proud and arrogant people decided to serve notice on those headmen helping the agent and the soldiers. On April 12 an assassin from his band murdered Tyee Jim, a friend of the white men. Three days later Tipsey's men ambushed and killed Edward Phillips, a miner on the Applegate.[27]

When these same warriors waylaid a packer in the Siskiyous in May, John Bonnycastle and a detachment from Fort Jones took up the pursuit. On the summit of the mountains thirty-eight DesChutes Indians, visiting in the area from central Oregon, joined Bonnycastle's regulars and searched with them east through the forest. The trail led into Cali-

---

[25] *Ibid.*, April 18, 1854.

[26] *Annual Report of the Commissioner of Indian Affairs, 1854*, 256, 295.

[27] *Oregon Statesman*, May 2, 1854. U. S. Congress, Senate, *Senate Misc. Doc. No. 59*, 36 Cong., 1 sess., 5.

fornia, and Bonnycastle feared that the Shastas from his own district were involved in the troubles. However, on the morning of May 20 the troops found their man—Tipsey was dead.

The refractory Oregon leader had entered a Shasta camp some thirty-six hours before and attempted to encourage these people to unite with him in his vendetta against the white men. The Shastas of Klamath River knew too well that they would only suffer should they act; so, instead of agreeing, they killed Tipsey, his son, and his son-in-law and waited for the regular troops to arrive.[28]

Bonnycastle praised the Shastas for their timely action and departed with his forces; the DesChutes Indians and volunteers remained in the camp. On the twenty-fourth these men, acting jointly, decided to force the Shastas to go to Fort Jones. They rounded up sixty people and drove the miserable refugees down river to Klamath Ferry. Here the Indians stopped to bathe. While five of them were in the water, their captors opened fire. The headman, "Bill," was shot, beaten, scalped, and, while still alive, thrown into the rapids. Terror-stricken, the women and children scrambled up the hillsides and, as the white men fired at them, tried to hide behind boulders and gnarled juniper trees. Bonnycastle, who later reported the massacre, reflected his judgment when he wrote: "An Indian from behind his bush fortunately shot and killed a whiteman named McKaney."[29]

As summer waned the Rogue country warmed and dried in its annual cycle; then thousands of grasshoppers moved through the valley, eating wheat, oats, melons, and vines and even stripping the oak trees of their leaves. These plagues warned the settlers that hard times were awaiting the immigrants soon to pass through Modoc territory on the Applegate Trail. Fearing that the Indians would renew their attacks on stragglers from the wagon trains, a company of volunteers,

[28] U. S. Congress, Senate, *Senate Exec. Doc. No. 16*, 33 Cong., 2 sess., 78–80.
[29] *Ibid.*, 81.

143

organized under the orders of Territorial Governor John W. Davis, left Jacksonville in August to patrol the route for three months. The men burned Indian villages, killed thirty to forty people, and returned to the Rogue Valley to file their claims for their services.[30]

In September, Joel Palmer, who had toured the region the previous spring, wrote his reports and emphasized the dismal future facing his Indian charges:

I found the Indians of the Rogue River Valley excited and unsettled. The hostilities of last summer had prevented the storing of the usual quantities of food; the occupation of their best root-grounds by the whites greatly abridged that resource; their scanty supplies and the unusual severity of the winter had induced disease, and death had swept away nearly one-fifth of those residing on the reserve. Consternation and dismay prevailed; many had fled, and others were preparing to fly to the mountains for security.[31]

Palmer clearly saw that one of the basic problems for the continuing crises and hostility between the white and aboriginal inhabitants of the Rogue Valley was the land situation. The Donation Land Act of 1850 and its subsequent modifications granted tracts of 640, 320, and 160 acres to qualified settlers. Some of the troubles in the Rogue country stemmed from the government's failure to clear Indian titles before allowing white men to take their claims. The Oregon problem was not a unique one—the land troubles had been part of the frontier experience since the first shiploads of immigrants landed on the eastern coast of the United States.[32]

Warfare, disease, and starvation had decimated the bands of valley people. The respected headman Aps-er-ka-har, known to many settlers as "Joe," died of tuberculosis in November.[33] The August, 1852, census had listed 1,154 Indians;

[30] *Journal of the Proceedings of the Council of the Legislative Assembly of Oregon Territory, Ninth Regular Session—1857–8*, 15–18.

[31] *Annual Report of the Commissioner of Indian Affairs, 1854*, 255.

[32] U. S. Congress, House, *House Exec. Doc. No. 93*, 34 Cong., 1 sess, 55–61.

[33] *Oregon Statesman*, Dec. 12, 1854.

a new survey of the survivors was made in the fall of 1854. The latter compilation located only 147 men; but two years before there were 406. The nine bands in 1854 totaled in all 523 people.[34]

Although many miners had rushed away to new strikes, Jacksonville prospered. Where Indian women had once swung their flails to shake seeds into their baskets and crouched on their hands and knees to gather acorns, there stood brick buildings, churches, and clapboard homes. And where those women had once lived were charred planks and open pits—the scars of warfare and destruction.

The Indians in the Rogue Valley struggled to survive another winter on the reservation. On the coast the Chetcos retreated from the mouth of the river to sites in the mountains more removed from the packers and travelers on the beach trails. The band living at the mouth of the Coquille was nearly extinct; survivors left the ruined village to join their neighbors up the river or north on Coos Bay.

[34] U. S. Congress, House, *House Exec. Doc. No. 93*, 34 Cong., 1 sess., 90.

6

THE WAR IN THE VALLEY

THE OLD MAN spoke slowly and haltingly; English was not easy for him. The persistent anthropologist continued to prod his hazy recollections of the past, and at last John Adams— for that was the name the agency schoolmaster had given him—spoke. His tale, a memory of life in 1855–56, was a fleeting glimpse into the tragedy of the last year the Rogues spent in their homeland. His account, simple but eloquent, speaks for itself:

Pretty rough times! Awful times when I'm baby. Rogue River Injun War that time. Well, soldier come, everybody scatter, run for hills. One family this way, one family other way. Some fighting. My father killed, my mother killed. Well, my uncle he come, my grandmother. Old woman, face like white woman, so old. "Well my poor mother, you old, not run. Soldiers coming close, we have to run fast. I not help it. I sorry. Must leave you here. Maybe soldiers not find you, we come back. Now this little baby, this my brother's baby. Two children I got myself. I sorry, I not help it. We leave this poor baby, too." That's what my uncle say.

Course, I small, maybe two years, maybe nearly three years. I not know what he say. Somebody tell me afterwards. Well, old grandmother cry, say: "I old, I not afraid die. Go ahead, get away from soldiers."

Well, most like dream, I 'member old grandmother pack me round in basket on her back. All time she cry and holler. I say, "Grandmother, what you do?"

"What is it, crying, grandmother?"

"I sorry for you, my child. Why I cry. I not sorry myself, I old.

147

You young, maybe somebody find you all right, you live."

Then I sleep long time. When I wake up, winter gone, spring time come. I 'member plenty flowers, everything smell good. Old grandmother sitting down, can't walk no more. Maybe rheumatism. She point long stick, say, "Pick that one, grandson."

I weak, can't walk. S'pose no eat long time.

I crawl on ground where she point. "This one, grandmother?"

"No, that other one."

"This one?"

"No, no! That one no good. That other one."

By in by I get right one, she say "Pull up, bring him here."

I crawl back, she eat part, give me part. Don't like it, me. Too sour. Well, she show me everything to eat, I crawl round, get roots. Pretty soon can walk. Old grandmother never walk. Just sit same place all time. . . .

One day hear something: "Pow! Pow!" She's too old for holler, me, I'm too small. Maybe I'm scared too. Well, I crawl inside tree and eat sugar. Pretty soon hear somebody talk. Then I'm 'fraid, hide in tree. Somebody coming! I lay down on ground, hide close. "Where are you? Where are you?" Well there's my uncle. He pick me up one hand. I 'member hanging over his arm while he go back my grandmother.

"Well," that man say, "soldiers not stay long that time. Pretty soon come back, can't find you. Think some grizzly-bear eat you. Look for bones, can't find bones. All winter I cry. Then I say my wife: "Maybe better go other side today. Maybe find something other side. . . . Then I look close. Little grass been moved. Pretty near can't see it. Some kind little foot been there! That how I find my old mother."

Pretty soon soldiers come again. That's the time they leave my old grandmother cause she can't walk, maybe she die right there, maybe soldiers kill her. She cry plenty when my uncle take me away. Well, all time going round in woods. After while my uncle get killed. Then I'm alone. Klamath Injun find me, bring me to new reservation.[1]

The final tragic months for the Indians of the Rogue

---

[1] Curtis, *The Hupa, Yurok, Karok, Wiyot, Tolowa and Tututni, Shasta, Klamath*, 93–95.

country opened in a familiar pattern. In May, 1855, a miner living in a lonely shanty on Indian Creek near the Klamath River was murdered. Supposing that the Takelmas of the Illinois Valley had committed the crime, two volunteer companies crossed the Siskiyous and marched down the narrow canyon of Althouse Creek to the mining town of Kerbyville. Their bloody mission of retribution left four Indian men and women killed. Only hours before, Dr. George Ambrose, the new Indian agent for the district, had anticipated troubles and had hurried several Indian families from the region to the safer reservation on the Rogue River.[2]

In July conflicts again occurred on the Klamath. Drunken Indians, trading for whisky with unscrupulous packers, forced a battle with a miner near the diggings on Humbug Creek. Killing this man, the Indians launched a two-day campaign of retribution and murdered eleven other miners along the Klamath, Scott, and Shasta rivers. While the volunteer companies formed again, Lieutenant Judah and some of the settlers near Fort Jones rounded up nearly one hundred peaceful Shasta people and brought them to the military post for protection. Those Indians remaining in the mountains became prey for the avengers.[3]

A chance event brought the Klamath troubles to the Rogue Valley. Six men who had temporarily left the Table Rock Reservation with passes issued by a justice of the peace in Jacksonville were on the Klamath when the killings began. Although they quickly returned to Oregon, the California miners had seen them and presumed they were guilty of the massacres.[4]

[2] *Oregon Statesman*, July 7, 1855.
[3] Among those murdered were John Pollock, William Hennessey, Edward Parrish, Peter Henrick, Thomas Gray, John L. Fickas, T. D. Matue, E. D. Matue, and two Mexicans named Ramon and Pedro. B. F. Dowell, "Oregon Indian War, Principally the War of 1855–56 in Southern Oregon" (MS), 32–39. U. S. Congress, House, *House Exec. Doc. No. 76*, 34 Cong., 3 sess., 92–93.
[4] *Oregon Statesman*, Aug. 18, Sept. 15, 1855.

The first week in August the volunteers arrived at Fort Lane and demanded that Captain Smith and Dr. Ambrose turn over the men they had seen. The commanders were willing to permit the Indians to be taken to Yreka for trial but declined to allow the volunteers to march onto the reservation to seize the suspects. Denied permission to show their prowess, the men resorted to calling a public meeting to voice their resentment of the officials. On August 5 several miners assembled at the cabins on Sterling Creek on the Applegate to hear the complaints. The volunteers resolved that unless they were given the six men within three days, they would forcibly seize them.[5]

Ambrose refused to accede to this ultimatum; yet, hoping to placate the angered men, he ordered two of the reservation Indians placed in irons at Fort Lane. The settlers in the Rogue Valley, including a correspondent of the *Oregon Statesman* who signed his articles "Truth," approved of the firm handling of the situation by Smith and Ambrose. The volunteers backed down and returned to California, where they showered the Yreka *Union* with their version of Indian affairs.[6]

A few warriors of Tipsey's band survived in their old haunts in the Siskiyous and foothills of the Cascades. In late August they stole a horse and, when its owner and his neighbors tracked them, ambushed their pursuers.[7] In September their petty thefts and acts multiplied. They burned fence rails at Vannoy's Ferry, stole boots and blankets from a settler named Walker, and shot three head of cattle at Tuft's Ranch.[8]

Ambrose, alarmed at the mounting resentment in the region, explained to Palmer the nature of the troubles:

[5] Ream, "Autobiographical Dictation," *loc. cit.*, 17.

[6] *Oregon Statesman*, Sept. 15, 1855.

[7] They killed Granville Keene and wounded Fred Alberding and T. Q. Taber. *Ibid.*, Sept. 22, 1855.

[8] U. S. Congress, House, *House Exec. Doc. No. 93*, 34 Cong., 1 sess., 63–64.

In most instances, the houses are of rude logs, and not very securely fastened, which offers a temptation to Indians hard for them to resist, especially when we consider they have been trained to steal from their infancy. After a repetition of thefts a few times, and the individual, after a hard day's work, has had to walk two or three miles to get his supper and lay in another small lot of provisions, which in a few days may probably go the same way, he gets peevish and angry, and embittered against the Indian race, and would about as soon shoot an Indian as eat his supper.[9]

Tipsey's men struck again on September 25, attacking teamsters in the Siskiyous. They overturned the wagons, killed two men, and chased the terrified survivors along the trail.[10] The next day a Shasta man reclaimed his wife, who had been held by a miner on Cottonwood Creek. He killed the prospector. When news of this act and the ambush in the Siskiyous reached Yreka, the volunteers mounted up.[11]

The region was ripe for serious hostilities; and, to add further to the uneasy situation, a prolonged dry spell had almost ended all mining operations. The animosities of a few settlers, the fears of many others, and the cruelty and hatred of unprincipled men fed the tensions that gripped the inhabitants of southern Oregon the first week of October. During those days court was in session in Jacksonville. This event, a ready excuse for any lonely pioneer to visit town, brought dozens of spectators and idlers into the settlement. Their grievances became boasts; and, fatefully for the Indians, the boasts were translated into action.

Self-proclaimed "Major" James Lupton, a packer who had come to Oregon with the Mounted Rifle Regiment in 1849, marched into Jacksonville with the Yreka volunteers. These men, still smarting from the rebuffs given them by the

[9] *Ibid.*, 63.

[10] Calvin Fields and John Cunningham were killed. Harrison B. Oatman, cousin of Olive Oatman, the famous Mohave captive, escaped to Jacksonville. *Oregon Statesman*, Oct. 13, 1855.

[11] *Ibid.* U. S. Congress, House, *House Exec. Doc. No. 93*, 34 Cong., 1 sess., 64–65.

151

agent and military officers in August, called a public meeting to sound out the Oregonians on exterminating the Indians. All looked bright for Lupton's deadly plan, and he consequently called a second get-together on October 7 to plan in greater detail the strategy for the massacre.[12]

Ostensibly the meeting was a quarterly church session, and two "elders" presided. In actuality, the assembly listened to a lengthy recitation of grievances against the Rogues. When the charges were almost exhausted, the chairman called for someone to speak on a religious subject. One brave man, firm in his convictions and calm in his demeanor, rose to address the audience. John Beeson, an immigrant from Illinois who had settled in the valley in 1853, urged all present, as Christians, to desist from the course so clearly laid out by the "exterminators." No one seconded Beeson's plea. His remarks were greeted with silence and, by some, with contempt.[13]

The meeting broke up, and as darkness lingered in the valley, the volunteers divided their forces for their destructive mission. Lupton led his company to an old Indian village on Butte Creek, a short distance from the reservation. The men found the survivors of "Jake's" band sleeping in their summer brush huts. They opened fire in the dark and massacred without quarter everyone they could find. They killed eight men—four of them aged—and fifteen women and children. The other company had less success; they only killed one woman and two small boys from "Sambo's" band.[14]

Charles Drew, quartermaster for the volunteers and long an apologist for any attempts to subdue the "savages," felt that the plan was "admirably executed." He only regretted that a larger number of Indians had not been killed. Drew ascribed this vexation to the Indian agent and officers at Fort

---

[12] Beeson, *A Plea For the Indians*, 47–48.

[13] *Ibid.*, 48.

[14] U. S. Congress, House, *House Exec. Doc. No. 93*, 34 Cong., 1 sess., 65–66. Dowell, "Oregon Indian War, Principally the War of 1855–56 in Southern Oregon," *loc. cit.*, 29.

Lane who had partially betrayed the volunteers by suspecting their intentions and advising the Indians to be vigilant.[15]

The Rogues struck back in reprisal. Too many memories of past wrongs and injustices, too many deaths from sickness, starvation, and murder had occurred for them to trust the white men again. On the reservation they murdered William Guin, an agency employee. Then, those too sick of war to continue the struggles sought protection from the understanding commander at Fort Lane. Their kinsmen who elected to fight grabbed their weapons and, filled with vengeance, fled the horrors of the valley.[16]

At dawn on October 9 the settlers living along the river between Gold Hill and Vannoy's Ferry near Grants Pass began another workday. The actions of Lupton's volunteers were unknown to them. The Rogues, pushing down river toward the wilderness in the coast mountains, first struck the Jacob B. Wagner ranch, where they murdered Wagner's wife and daughter and left the body of Miss Sarah Pellett, a temperance lecturer on her way to Jacksonville, in the smoldering ruins.[17]

At a nearby ranch, George W. Harris was splitting shingles in the yard while his wife was behind the house washing clothes. Harris looked up to see Indians pouring out of the forest and running toward him. He seized his rifle and ran with the family for the cabin but was shot as he attempted to close the door. Mechanically he fired his gun twice, staggered across the room, and fainted. Sophie, his eleven-year-old daughter, ran to the door and was shot through the arm. Harris' wife barred the entrance and, when her husband revived, followed

[15] In the chaos on Butte Creek, Lupton received a fatal arrow through the lungs. Several other volunteers were wounded—many of them by their comrades. Dowell, "Oregon Indian War, Principally the War of 1855–56 in Southern Oregon," *loc. cit.*

[16] Agent Ambrose wrote on October 9 that "Elijah's" and "Sam's" people, in spite of the attack of the volunteers, remained peaceful. They helped protect the agency property and personnel. U. S. Congress, House, *House Exec. Doc. No. 93*, 34 Cong., 1 sess., 66–67.

[17] *Oregon Statesman*, Oct. 20, 1855.

his instructions and loaded his pistols; but, to her anguish and despair, he died. Alone with a wounded daughter, with Indians yelling and burning the outbuildings on the farm, and fearful for her small son somewhere out in the fields, she defended the cabin for over five hours. When the Indians left, the woman hid with her daughter in the forest until the troops found her the next morning.[18]

There were other massacres that day. Frank Reed, the Harris' hired man, and David Harris were murdered near the cabin. The Rogues killed four people at the Haines place. J. K. Jones and his wife were murdered, although their children escaped. The Indians also killed Isaac Shelton at Evans Ferry, a man named Hamilton at the river crossing near Jewett's claim, and four teamsters hauling apple trees for a nursery company in the Willamette Valley.[19]

As news of the outbreak spread through southwestern Oregon, the people fell back on the old pattern of defenses. Many refugees streamed into Jacksonville, while other miners and settlers, refusing to abandon their claims, built palisades and dug trenches around cabins. Their makeshift quarters are remembered as Fort Birdseye, Fort Vannoy, Six Bit House, and Fort Bailey. On October 10 the families living along Cow Creek in the Umpqua territory formed a company of volunteers to stand guard at the entrance to the canyon to prevent hostile parties from passing through to the settlements to the north. Four days after Lupton's "exterminators" struck the Rogues, John E. Ross, acting under a resolution by the Americans collected at Jacksonville, commissioned a regiment of volunteers. By October 14 he had enlisted about five hundred men in nine companies.[20]

Before a week had passed, the authorities in the Wil-

[18] *Ibid.*

[19] *Ibid.* Dowell, "Oregon Indian War, Principally the War of 1855–56 in Southern Oregon" *loc. cit.*, 33–39. U. S. Congress, Senate, *Senate Misc. Doc. No. 59*, 36 Cong., 1 sess., 7.

[20] *Oregon Statesman*, Oct. 20, 1855. U. S. Congress, Senate, *Senate Misc. Doc. No. 59*, 36 Cong., 1 sess., 30.

lamette Valley approved direct action to cope with the hostilities. Joel Palmer amended the regulations he was forwarding to his agents. He ordered them to bring immediately the Cow Creek bands of Umpquas to the reservation called for in the treaties signed in 1853 and 1854. Edward P. Drew, whose district extended from the mouth of the Umpqua to Coos Bay, and Benjamin Wright, on the southern coast, were requested to round up their charges if they thought such a move necessary. The adjutant general of Oregon Territory, by governor's order, called for the mustering of two battalions of mounted volunteers in central and southern Oregon to keep open the roads. He directed these men to select their own officers.[21]

On October 17 the Rogues besieged a cabin and temporary breastwork of earth and flour sacks at a miner's camp near Skull Bar at the mouth of Galice Creek. The bands under "George" and "Limpy," people who usually lived near the mouth of the Applegate, fought desperately for over eight hours with more than forty miners and packers. The Indians, attempting to dislodge these men who held a key position on the river trail, continued the unsuccessful struggle until sundown, when they retreated, dragging their dead and wounded with them. The miners suffered fifteen casualties, four of whom later died.[22]

On the twenty-fourth the Rogues attacked supply wagons and hog drovers on Cow Creek, killing Hollen Bailey. They found no opposition and consequently swept down the creek burning cabins, barns, and fences, and driving retreating pioneers from the valley. One settler named Redfield carried his wounded wife on his back as he fled, for the Indians had killed both horses pulling his wagon.[23]

The next day, farther down the Umpqua, a company of

[21] U. S. Congress, House, *House Exec. Doc. No. 93*, 34 Cong., 1 sess., 4, 73–74.

[22] Those killed were J. W. Pickett, Samuel Sanders, Israel Adams, and Benjamin Tufts. *Oregon Statesman*, Nov. 3, 1855. U. S. Congress, Senate, *Senate Misc. Doc. No. 59*, 36 Cong., 1 sess., 31–33.

[23] *Oregon Statesman*, Nov. 3, 1855.

volunteers attacked a village of peaceful Indians at Looking Glass Prairie. These people, who thought they were safe among their white neighbors, suffered at least five deaths— four men and one woman.[24] To the south, Agent Ambrose was more successful in thwarting the "exterminators." He had 303 Indians at Fort Lane; most of them were from "Sam's" and "Elijah's" bands. The regular army troops protected them from the volunteers.[25]

John Ross selected Camp Stewart as volunteer headquarters. He ordered supplies, enlisted men, sent pack trains to Yreka and Crescent City for ammunition and weapons, and prepared for the campaign while trying to maintain a semblance of co-ordination of the companies in the field. The responsibilities thrust upon any commander in time of war are burdensome enough, but a man commanding volunteers made up of rabble and malcontents who elect their own officers has more than his share of problems. In late October the following "express," now surviving as a folded, tobacco-stained page with a faded ink message, arrived at Camp Stewart:

SIR: The Pack Animal that you furnished me to transport government stores to the Army the last i saw of it was going over the Divide between Jackass Creek & town [Jacksonville]. Head up tail Curled over her back & going at about twenty two feet. government stores flying over the tops of Pine trees. I Holoed go it ole gal your on the right road to the Army. . . .

Your most Obedient
D. M. TEXARS
Applegate Rangers[26]

Confusion reigned in the heart of the Rogue country. At Althouse and Sucker creeks in the Siskiyous the miners hur-

---

[24] *Ibid.*

[25] U. S. Congress, House, *House Exec. Doc. No. 93,* 34 Cong., 1 sess., 89.

[26] Dowell, "Oregon Indian War, Principally the War of 1855–56 in Southern Oregon," *loc. cit.,* 71.

riedly held citizens' meetings, formed a company of soldiers, and began scouring the hills for the Indians who were ambushing the pack trains from the coast. No sooner had the volunteers left their camps than the Indians fired the shanties, tenpin alleys, card houses, and piles of whipsawed lumber.[27] At Deer Creek on the Umpqua, volunteer companies coming from the Willamette Valley established their temporary headquarters. The small settlement hummed with activity late into the night as blacksmiths fixed shoes for the mounts and farm-boys-turned-soldier played poker.[28]

In the midst of these activities and troubles a surveying party from Port Orford was at last opening a trail through the coast range. Nearly four years had passed since the search for a route had begun. T'Vault's explorations ended in massacre on the Coquille. Lieutenant Williamson was also unable to find a practical route, although he had noted and mapped many of the land features. Now, in late October, Lieutenant August V. Kautz and a troop detachment approached the Oregon–California trail after a thirteen-day trip from the coast.

On October 24 the soldiers from Fort Orford, vaguely aware that war might be under way with the Indians, followed the mountain ridges through the forest toward Grave Creek. The expedition had turned back from the Big Bend of the Rogue ten days earlier when it found the miners there fortified and fighting the Indians. After acquiring more arms and ammunition at Fort Orford, the survey party resumed its march. Within two or three miles of the Oregon-California trail, the Rogues ambushed the soldiers. Young Lieutenant Kautz fell to the ground, clutching his chest. His detachment started to run, thinking him killed, but fortunately the ball had struck his pocket diary and incapacitated him only temporarily. His retreating troops turned and managed to crash

[27] Reinhart, *The Golden Frontier*, 97–98. Dowell, "Oregon Indian War, Principally the War of 1855–56 in Southern Oregon," *loc. cit.*, 123.
[28] *Oregon Statesman*, Nov. 3, 1855.

out of the forest to reach Fort Lane. They left behind several pack animals and two dead privates, Gill and Adams.[29]

Kautz's survey party had made an awesome discovery. It had stumbled into the hideout of the warring Indians. When this information was reported, Captain Smith notified the volunteers at nearby Camp Stewart. Acting within hours, Smith set out with 105 regulars. Ross brought his troops then present while two companies from Douglas County set out to rendezvous with the forces at the crossing of Grave Creek.

The 250 men marched into the rugged hills south of the trail, traversed the ridges, and—after three hours in the field near the place the troops from Fort Orford had been attacked—spied the Indians on a high mountain ridge. The volunteers, armed with sabers, pistols, squirrel guns, and almost anything they could call a weapon, eagerly rushed forward. When they were three-quarters of a mile from the Rogues, they saw the armed warriors waiting for them at the summit of a bald peak. With a wild cry and great disorder the men threw their coats and blankets into the brush and charged their foe in a fatal advance.

The Indians held their ground and raked the volunteers with a deadly barrage of arrows and bullets. They turned the charge and forced the men down the mountain in scrambling retreat. The battle which had opened near ten in the morning continued throughout the day with sporadic firing, but the white men did not attempt another suicidal assault. At dark the troops withdrew to find water for their wounded and dying. All was quiet for a few hours until an accidental pistol shot stampeded the camp. The cries of scared men, wild firing of guns into the dark night, and fear that they were being attacked—all contributed to the confusion in which one man was killed and two were wounded.[30]

At dawn, November 1, the Rogues surrounded the

[29] *Alta California*, Jan. 3, 1856. Crook, *General George Crook: His Autobiography*, 29. Gibson, *Efforts of Speech and Pen*, 16–24.
[30] *Oregon Statesman*, Nov. 24, 1855.

soldiers' camp and rushed it, hoping to rout their enemy, but were forced back after nearly four hours of battle. The volunteers and regulars were in a very dangerous situation. Most of the men had not slept for nearly forty-eight hours; sufficient provisions had not been procured; water was almost impossible to find. The commanders ordered retreat, litters were rigged to carry the wounded from the field, and the ragged forces trudged out of the hills. The government troops stayed two days at temporary Camp Allaston on Grave Creek to bury their dead and prepare to move their injured men. The volunteers took their wounded to Six Bit House, a tavern and inn on Wolf Creek. The battle of Hungry Hill had been a costly campaign—seven volunteers killed, twenty wounded, and four regulars killed, seven wounded. The Rogues, who perhaps lost twenty warriors, were left in control of a section of their homeland.[31]

As the motley volunteers straggled into the temporary hospital and headquarters at Six Bit House, a government survey crew under Lieutenant Henry L. Abbot reached the place. Abbot's party, making the Oregon-California reconnaissance for the Pacific Railroad surveys, could scarcely believe the confusion of the Oregon Mounted Volunteers. Lieutenant George Crook, who was escorting the expedition, wrote a few lines about Laban Buoy, a stout volunteer leader armed with an old artillery sword:

He drew his little sword with his left hand, and brandished it over his head, and bawled out, "Tenshun the company!" Some answered back, "Go to Hell!" while others said, "Hold it, Cap, until I go to the rear," only in not such choice language.

"Now," says he, "at the command 'prepare to mount,' catch your horses by the bridle with your left hand, put your foot in the stirrup, and mount." Suiting the action to the word, in attempt-

---

[31] The volunteers killed were Henry Pearl, Jacob W. Miller, John Gillespie, Jonathan Pettigrew, Charles Goodwin, John Kennedy, and John Winters. *Oregon Statesman*, Nov. 24, 1855. Dowell, "Oregon Indian War, Principally the War of 1855–56 in Southern Oregon," *loc. cit.*, 169–71.

ing to mount, his foot slipped out of the stirrup and his chin struck the pommel of the saddle and his corposity shook like a bag of jelly. He looked about at some of the men who were on their horses, when he said, "That's right boys, get up thar."[32]

As the first weeks in November passed, the Indians made brief forays into the valley, fired on express riders in the mountains, and burned abandoned cabins, but remained mostly hidden in the canyons and forests where the Rogue Canyon cuts into the coast range. The volunteers left their headquarters at Camp Stewart and moved down the river to a position nearer the field of action at Fort Vannoy. On November 9, Colonel Ross mustered out of service four volunteer companies whom he had enlisted and enrolled them in a new battalion as ordered by Governor George Curry.[33]

Other companies of volunteers who did not come to the reorganization were deployed to the north to keep open the trail. Joseph Bailey's men from Lane County went to Camas Valley on the headwaters of the Coquille River. Samuel Gordon's company was stationed near the mouth of Cow Creek. A detachment under T. W. Prath guarded the Indians living along the South Umpqua. Captain Jonathan Keeney's men established Camp Bailey, a site about five miles south of Cow Creek crossing, where they could guard the road through the Grave Creek Hills. Buoy and Hardy Eliff took their men to Grave Creek.[34]

Thus with volunteers scattered throughout the region and a fair amount of supplies collected for a campaign, Major James Bruce, former compatriot in arms with "exterminator" Lupton and now commander of the southern battalion, met on November 17 with Henry Judah of the United States regulars. Since they believed the Indians to be moving down river, the commanders decided to follow them and, if possible, overwhelm the Rogues in the mountains. The expeditionary

[32] Crook, *General George Crook: His Autobiography*, 26–27.
[33] U. S. Congress, Senate, *Senate Misc. Doc. No. 59*, 36 Cong., 1 sess., 32.
[34] *Table Rock Sentinel*, Dec. 22, 1855.

forces departed on the twenty-first, Judah taking his men and three companies of volunteers to the Grave Creek crossing where they turned toward the Rogue River. Two companies of volunteers, planning to tighten the vise of soldiers pushing against the Indians, started directly downstream.

These forces marched into the most isolated part of the Rogue country. On November 23, Judah's men camped near the mouth of Whiskey Creek on the Rogue River and the next day hiked a dozen miles along the ridges above the canyon until they arrived at the Little Meadows near sunset. Thick brush, fallen timber, and the narrow ridge trails were hazardous and fatiguing for the regulars and volunteers. They found that Little Meadows was like many of the open tablelands in the mountains along the river. The forest suddenly opened on luxuriant, grass-covered fields holding scattered swampy basins filled with sphagnum and flycatcher plants.

The soldiers had pushed on to this destination, for they knew that there the horses could find pasture and thought the Rogues might be camped nearby. As the men crossed the prairie they saw the glow of campfires some five or six miles away on the riverbank. The leaders concluded that these were the dinner fires of the volunteers marching down the river to meet them. To their surprise, however, the volunteers who had left Fort Vannoy on the river route trudged into Little Meadows late that night. Finding the canyon nearly impassable, they had forded the river at Whiskey Creek and followed the other troops.[35]

The soldiers then realized that they had found the Indian stronghold. On Sunday the twenty-fifth Bruce sent spies to observe the enemy. They reported that some 150 men and their families were fortified at the lower end of a bar in the river at a very narrow portion of the canyon. The spies emphasized that the Indians held a nearly impregnable position, for the riverbank on the southern side was densely forested

[35] *Ibid.*

161

while on the north crumbling, precipitous spur ridges fell at right angles to the stream. The commanders knew the terrain well, for they had crossed part of it to reach Little Meadows.

In spite of these obstacles the soldiers set out on the twenty-sixth to attack the Rogues. Judah's regulars, dragging a heavy howitzer, and several detachments of volunteers, numbering in all 146 men, planned to approach the enemy camp from the north. They had made their way almost half the distance to their goal when an express message from Major Bruce caused them to turn back.[36]

Bruce, commanding 286 men, had marched to the river some three miles below the Indians' camp and had begun to build rafts for crossing in hope that his men could march up the south side of the Rogue to catch the Indians in a cross fire. The chopping of wood for the rafts immediately warned the Rogues of the soldiers' intentions, and, before a raft was launched, they opened fire on the volunteers. The riverbank scarcely provided sufficient rocks and trees for the scrambling volunteers. The parties exchanged shots throughout the day, and four white men were wounded and one killed. The Indians, repulsing more than five times their number, suffered two or three casualties.[37]

Thus the Rogues turned back another expedition, although not as decisively as in their victory at Hungry Hill. By November 27 the soldiers had only three days' rations remaining, and threatening signs of a coming winter storm clouded the sky. Some of the troops were without shoes and sufficient blankets for the cold nights. The commanders discontinued the war and marched their men back to their headquarters at Fort Lane and Camp Leland, a new volunteer base on Grave Creek.[38]

[36] *Ibid.*

[37] William Lewis bled to death on the riverbank. *Ibid.* Dowell, "Oregon Indian War, Principally the War of 1855–56 in Southern Oregon," *loc. cit.*, 50. *Oregon Statesman*, Dec. 8, 1855.

[38] *Table Rock Sentinel*, Dec. 22, 1855.

In the valley 314 Indians camped at Fort Lane. They possessed no rifles but were allowed to keep their digging sticks, bows, and arrows. Nearly 300 others waited under an agent's charge on the Umpqua. All these people lacked food, proper shelter, and clothing. To make matters worse, many were sick and dying from tuberculosis, measles, and malnutrition.[39]

Superintendent Palmer had anticipated these problems and in the fall had explored possible reservation sites along the north central Oregon coast in the vicinity of the Siletz River and on the east side of the coast range along the Yamhill. When he found that all but twenty-five land owners in the Yamhill region would sell their lands to the government, he pushed ahead with his plans to remove the peaceful bands from the Rogue country.[40]

However, before Palmer acted, some of the hostile Umpquas attacked the cabins of Rice, Robinson, Richards, Fisher, Newland, and Wells near Looking Glass Creek in Douglas County. On December 1 they killed hogs and chickens, fired outbuildings and vacant cabins, stole horses and mules, and chased several pioneer families from their homes. A company of volunteers found their camp near Olalla and fought them on the fourth of December, killing two men and wounding several.[41]

As Christmas neared, the weather in the Rogue Valley became increasingly colder. Snow piled up to eighteen inches. Sleigh parties went out from Jacksonville for winter rides through the open fields in the valley, and crews cut blocks of ice to store in cellars for the coming summer. The temper-

---

[39] *Ibid.*, Dec. 1, 1855. U. S. Congress, House, *House Exec. Doc. No. 93*, 34 Cong., 1 sess., 109–10.

[40] U.S. Congress, House, *House Exec. Doc. No. 93*, 34 Cong., 1 sess., 85–86.

[41] *Table Rock Sentinel*, Dec. 22, 1855. *Oregon Statesman*, Jan. 8, 1856. Riddle, *Early Days in Oregon*, 98–104.

[42] *Alta California*, Jan. 19, 1856.

ature dropped so low that the Rogue froze over at Vannoy's Ferry, and men and animals were able to walk across.[42]

As the freezing winds whistled through the rude shelters of the Indians camped near the reservation, the "exterminators" struck again. On Christmas Eve, 1855, two companies of volunteers under Alcorn and Rice marched to Butte Creek, where "Jake's" people had been massacred the previous October. The commanders had visited the two villages the day before and assured the Rogues of their peace and friendship but were actually scouting for the attack. They murdered nineteen men, burned the supplies and houses, and left the surviving women and children to starve and die of exposure in the snow.[43]

The next week Rice's volunteers and twenty-five infantrymen from Fort Lane departed for the Applegate, where the Indians were living in abandoned cabins. On January 2, 1856, when the expedition was crossing through the hills behind Jacksonville, the Indians poured a few random shots into the line of march. They downed Martin Angel, one of the ruffians who had screamed for extermination in 1853. The soldiers continued on to the river but were unable to attack the Indians because a mule carrying the ammunition for the howitzer fell over a cliff and drowned in a deep pool in the stream. More ammunition arrived on January 5, and during the day the men exchanged shots with the fortified Indians. Firing the cannon into the cabins failed to dislodge the enemy, and they escaped during the night. The Rogues killed Dr. W. Myers but lost three of their own men. Throughout January the volunteers patrolled the region, searching for the survivors of "John's" band.[44]

After the first of the year volunteers searched the hillsides and ravines along Cow Creek and other tributaries of the Umpqua. They had little success in locating their elusive

[43] *Oregon Statesman*, Jan. 15, 1855. U. S. Congress, House, *House Exec. Doc. No. 93*, 34 Cong., 1 sess., 48.

[44] *Alta California*, Jan. 18, 1856. *Oregon Statesman*, Jan. 15, 1856.

enemy, but the Indians knew where they were. On the evening of January 23, Joseph Bailey's men camped on a prairie in the mountains near Cow Creek. They posted no sentries, and while the men were wrestling and lounging about their fires the Umpquas let loose a barrage which killed two men.[45]

In the meantime, Palmer was rapidly pushing ahead with his plans for Indian removal. The superintendent's ideas were not readily accepted by the residents of the Willamette Valley. In January thirty-five members of the territorial House of Representatives and Council signed a petition calling for Palmer's removal on three counts: he recognized illegitimate chiefs when signing treaties; he was bringing "thousands of Indians from remote parts of the country" to colonize them near the heart of the valley; and he had joined the Know-Nothings.[46]

The Oregon politicos did not stop with criticizing and urging the removal of the Indian superintendent. They adopted a memorial for the recall of General John Wool, commander of the Pacific Department of the United States Army. Wool's problems were tremendous. To the north he had several companies of regulars fighting the Indians of Washington Territory, in southern Oregon there were increasingly complex military problems and too few troops, and worst of all there was constant friction between the regular troops and the volunteers. The legislature charged Wool with inactivity: refusing to send out troops to relieve the volunteers, refusing to supply the volunteers with men and ammunition, and going into winter quarters when the war was unsettled.[47]

In almost every case, in spite of the many columns of print in territorial newspapers, Wool's actions were justifiable. He needed more time to obtain additional companies of regulars before deploying his forces in the field. He needed to

[45] Thomas S. Gage and John L. Gardner died in the ambush. *Oregon Statesman*, Feb. 5, 1856. Riddle, *Early Days in Oregon*, 106.

[46] U. S. Congress, House, *House Exec. Doc. No. 93*, 34 Cong., 1 sess., 133-35.

[47] *Oregon Statesman*, Feb. 12, 1856.

wait until the winter snow melted before deciding upon supply routes and launching campaigns. He well knew the murderous and extermination-minded tactics of the disorderly volunteers —the same men who charged up so tremendous a bill for their services in the war of 1853.

In spite of vociferous opposition, Palmer began in late January to remove the Umpquas. By the second week in February, 480 people from the Umpqua, Mollalla, and Calapuya Indian bands had reached the Grande Rhonde Reservation on the Yamhill.[48] At last, when military protection was obtained, 400 Indians left the Table Rock reserve in the Rogue Valley for the long march through the snow-covered mountains to their new home near the Willamette Valley. As the Indians passed the settlement on Deer Creek on the Umpqua, one of the residents there wrote to the *Statesman* his advice for their treatment on the reservation:

We would suggest that a few school-masters be distributed among them—and the subject of agriculture be *whaled* into them sufficiently to enable them to raise their own beans, and potatoes —the use of the plow, and the spade should be taught them, enough of the use of the latter, at least, to dig their own graves.[49]

Thus ended the disastrous and bloody war. The many thefts of the renegades of Tipsey's band of Shastas and the inhumane massacres of the volunteers had caused troubles which cost the lives of hundreds of people, destroyed large amounts of property, and inflicted suffering, which, for the Indians, would continue for many more years on a lonely and distant reservation.

The end had come for the Rogues of the valley. The pitiful survivors marched the long two hundred miles to the north, leaving the unburied bones of their mothers, fathers, brothers, sisters, and children.

---

[48] *Ibid. Alta California*, Feb. 22, 1856.
[49] U. S. Congress, House, *House Exec. Doc. No. 93*, 34 Cong., 1 sess., 48. *Oregon Statesman*, March 25, 1856.

In the mountains to the west, along the canyon of the Rogue, were the confused and hostile survivors of the troubles in the valley. These broken families had not had time to collect acorns or preserve sufficient salmon from the fall runs. Scattered behind them were their tools and baskets, their woodpecker scalps and deerskins, and their strings of long white dentalium shells. In the snowbound hills they huddled around fires or shared crowded plank houses with bands whose villages had not yet been destroyed.

7

THE WAR ON THE COAST

THE COAST INDIANS had to a large extent escaped the agonies that befell their kinsmen and neighbors in the heartland of the Rogue country. Indeed, most of them still occupied their old homes. Although many of these people had abandoned animal skins for cotton clothing, they had little changed their life patterns. Their access to guns was limited, but their inventiveness found ready use for new materials. The men and boys armed their arrows with finely chipped points of glass or razor-sharp metal. The women stashed dried fish in castoff biscuit tins and shipping kegs as well as their baskets.

Whims of a Congress a continent away had left the legal title to this land, at least temporarily, with its original inhabitants. In spite of the treaties and agreements forwarded to Washington, D.C., by agents and superintendents, no documents relating to the territory between the Umpqua and the Chetco had been ratified in the Senate. To correct this ambiguity and to answer the demands of settlers and town promoters like William Tichenor, in August, 1855, Joel Palmer came to the mouth of the Rogue River. At the treaty grounds near the large Tututni village some three miles upstream from the ocean, Palmer and a detachment of troops from Fort Orford waited for the Indians to assemble.

From the villages of the Shasta Costa far up the river, from the bands living at Oak Flats on the Illinois, from the realm of the Mikonotunnes near the riffles below Copper Canyon, and from the many villages north and south along

169

the coast, the Rogues gathered for the conference. Nearly a thousand Indians, including old women with soot-tattooed chins and proud young boys dressed in nothing but soldiers' castoff caps or shirts, assembled for the deliberations. Palmer had worked diligently to attract these people for another round of treaty talks. He had dispatched runners to all villages carrying the news of distribution of blankets, hatchets, and beads.

The discussions were about to begin when a quarrel between an Indian and a miner resulted in bloodshed. Palmer quickly arrested the young Indian but allowed the miner, more wounded in pride than in body, to return home. Fearing that the rabble in the nearby shanty towns would try to lynch his prisoner, the superintendent entrusted him to the regular troops. As a detachment was taking the Indian up river to the council grounds, a canoe stealthily drew alongside in the darkness, and the pursuers fired a volley at the prisoner, killing him. The troops returned the shots and killed three avenging miners.[1]

The Rogues, alarmed and angered at the death of another of their people, fled the council site. The miners formed a vigilance committee and threatened to attack both the soldiers and the Indians, holding them all responsible for the death of their three cronies. The situation appeared ominous, but Palmer's counsel and cool thinking prevailed. He soon reassembled the Rogues and affixed the names of their headmen to a treaty, another to be ignored by the Senate.[2]

All was quiet on the coast until October, when repercussions of the war in the valley spread down the canyon. The first indications of impending hostilities came at the Big Bend, the meadow deep in the coast mountains where T'Vault's lost explorers had turned north to the Coquille.

[1] The murderers in the night were James Pluford, Watt Hankton, and Michael O'Brien. *Oregon Statesman*, Sept. 15, 22, 1855. Tichenor, "Among the Oregon Indians," *loc. cit.*, 31, 35–36. Glisan, *A Journal of Army Life*, 240–54.
[2] Glisan, *A Journal of Army Life*, 240–54.

Randolph Tichenor, Charles Foster, John Mast, and a few other hardy miners living there found their Indian neighbors suddenly absent. Within a few days the Rogues attacked these prospectors. Foster and Tichenor fortified their primitive settlement and anticipated renewed troubles when, on October 14, Lieutenant August Kautz and his road-survey crew reached the Big Bend. Although the soldiers provided the miners with additional ammunition and supplies, prudence won out; the men left their isolated claims and fell back to the coast settlements.[3]

The withdrawal of these men, rumors that two women had been killed on the trail between Crescent City and Kerbyville, and accounts of the massacres in the Rogue Valley alarmed and panicked the people living on the coast. The miners who yet courted fortune at Whiskey Run abandoned their sluices and fled to Empire City on Coos Bay. Although the Coos Indians had always been peaceful, the settlers and the refugees constructed a stockade one hundred feet square with a fourteen-foot-high palisade. For several weeks they retreated to their two-story blockhouse which overlooked the bay.[4]

Fewer men with families lived at Gold Beach and Prattsville. Consequently the Curry County pioneers took less deliberate action to prepare for war. When the first news of the troubles arrived, they started to build forts on both the north and south banks of the Rogue at its mouth, but these ventures were halfhearted. The men abandoned the work when the warring Indians did not appear.[5]

No doubt the restraint of the Tututni, the Chetcos, and the Coquille peoples was in part ascribable to the vigorous efforts of Benjamin Wright. In spite of his faults and past

[3] Dodge, *Pioneer History of Coos and Curry Counties, Oregon*, 92. Glisan, *A Journal of Army Life*, 258.
[4] Sengstacken, *Destination West!*, 148. Dement, "After the Covered Wagons," *loc. cit.*, 20–21.
[5] Dodge, *Pioneer History of Coos and Curry Counties, Oregon*, 362.

reputation, Wright worked hard to maintain peace. Robert Dunbar, collector of customs at Port Orford, wrote: "Ben is on the jump day and night." And truly he was, for the agent hurried back and forth along the coast trails reminding the Indians of their treaties and counseling the miners on their need for caution.[6]

Of greatest concern to the agent were the "fire-eaters," the coast version of the "exterminators." These forces nearly seized the initiative on the upper Coquille River. No sooner had the settlers rushed their families from that area than the Indians swept down the middle and south branches of the river. On October 21 they burned the cabin of Abraham Hoffman. Some young miners and farmers who refused to be driven out of their new homes forted up at the cabins of William Rowland and Ephraim Catching.[7]

On November 7 these men formed the Coquille Guard, an extralegal volunteer company headquartered at Catching's claim. Nineteen men swore to obey David Hall, the subagent appointed for the region by Ben Wright. Hall attempted to round up all the Coquilles in the area and hold them on a temporary reservation on the south fork. These people, no doubt remembering the expedition against them by Colonel Casey in 1851 and the massacre of the Nasomah band in 1854, were reluctant to gather, but many finally came to the reserve.[8]

The Coquille Guard marched up and down the river throughout November and December, worked on their quarters at Fort Kitchen, and skirmished briefly with the Indians. They killed four men in battle and hanged another. Wright rode into their camp on Christmas Eve and ordered the volunteers to disperse and end their aggressions. The officers reluctantly discharged their company the last day of January.

[6] U. S. Congress, House, *House Exec. Doc. No. 93*, 34 Cong., 1 sess., 127–28.

[7] John Alva Harry, "Diary, 1854–56" (MS).

[8] Dodge, *Pioneer History of Coos and Curry Counties, Oregon*, 97.

Wright returned to Port Orford, taking with him many of the Coquilles, who were never to return to their old homes.[9]

Meanwhile the valley Indians, driven through the mountains by the soldiers during the November campaign, moved closer to the coast. Their presence, made more sinister by rumor and uncertainty, kept the settlers uneasy with fear of attack. In January, 1856, when two miners were killed about forty miles up the Rogue from the mouth of the river, troops from Fort Orford moved into the region to attempt to stem the influx of refugees.

Lieutenants John Chandler and John Drysdale took seventeen men to the junction of the Illinois and the Rogue. Their mission was twofold: to find Enos—a Canadian Indian who was guiding the murdered miners—and to urge the peaceful bands to withdraw to the coast. The search for Enos was unsuccessful, for the former guide for John Frémont simply hid in the forest when the soldiers neared his village. When the young lieutenants were not able to induce the peaceful bands to leave their plank houses for the uncertainties of life near the settlements, the troops fell back to the towns at the mouth of the river.[10]

An uneasy calm marked the monotonous winter days. Storms from the southwest came as usual to the region, and the twenty inches of rain which fell in December sluiced out the creeks and rivers. Far upstream the volunteers gambled away their days at Camp Leland. The regular troops escorted the surviving valley Indians to their new reservation. Chandler and Drysdale quitted Prattsville and returned to Fort Orford, but the Gold Beach Guard, a volunteer company determined to watch the Indians on the lower river, stationed itself across from the Tututni village at the treaty grounds.

The presence of the armed volunteers and the reports of brutality and massacre from up the river undermined what little confidence the Tututni had in their white neighbors.

9 Harry, "Diary, 1854–56," *loc. cit.* "Notes on Coos Bay," *loc. cit.*, 32–35.
10 *Alta California*, Feb. 5, 1856. Glisan, *A Journal of Army Life*, 269–81.

For more than four years their women had been prey to lusty frontiersmen. When young men and agitators like Enos counseled war, all restraint was abandoned. The coast warriors decided to strike first and set the night of February 22 for their campaign.[11]

The Tututni planned their strategy well, for most of the settlers and miners along the beaches between Cape Sebastian and Euchre Creek assembled in Gold Beach that evening to celebrate George Washington's birthday with an all-night dance. As the fiddlers played old tunes, the pioneers frolicked, drank, and made merry. When the party was well under way, the Indians launched their attack.

Near dawn they struck the camp of the Gold Beach Guard. Of the fourteen men present, they felled nine in the initial onslaught. Five of the volunteers dashed into the brush and managed to escape; one of the survivors, Charles Foster, ran most of two days to find refuge in Port Orford. A canoe filled with partygoers heading home from the celebration stopped in the river when the musket shots echoed through the hills. The people drifted with the current so that they might listen more closely. When they heard the cries of the Tututni and the dying screams of the volunteers, they turned about and paddled madly down river.[12]

The terrified pioneers carried news of the hostilities to the crowd still at the dance hall in Gold Beach. The weary people awakened their children, grabbed what food and arms they could find, and rushed to the riverbank. As the new day dawned, they anxiously ferried across the Rogue to seek refuge in the half-completed structure which they heralded as Fort Miner. Fortunately for the refugees, Michael Riley and Dr. D. S. Holton had persisted in their efforts to build a stockade. The two men had hauled logs from the beach to a nearby swampy field. There amidst clumps of tussock and wild iris they had built two small cabins and surrounded them

[11] Glisan, *A Journal of Army Life*, 268, 282.
[12] Dodge, *Pioneer History of Coos and Curry Counties, Oregon*, 73, 282.

with an earthen rampart. The refugees worked with a frenzy and within hours mounded the soil about their retreat into a sturdy embankment.[13]

The Rogue's attack was a deadly success. In their sweep through the pioneer settlements they killed twenty-three persons, many of them members of the volunteer company raised to defend this section of the river. They burned nearly every building they found and fired most of the town of Gold Beach. With the settlers and miners confined to their rude fort, the Indians were again masters of their homeland.[14]

The uprising brought tragedy to a German immigrant family living at Elizabethtown, the cluster of mining shanties six miles up the coast from Gold Beach. The Indians swarmed into the cabin of John Geisel and murdered him and his three small sons. After burning the settlement they spirited away the horrified widow, Christina, her fourteen-year-old daughter Mary, and her infant child Anne.[15]

Another victim felled by the Rogues was Benjamin Wright. Ben and John Poland, the leader of the Guard, were at a cabin just below the treaty grounds when the Indians struck. The Tututni gave the men no quarter. Wright's intemperance, mistreatment of Indian women, and his notorious past were more than enough to mark him as a dead man. Of the dozen different accounts of his death, each indicates that the murderers mutilated his body.[16]

The sleepy garrison at Port Orford came to life when Charles Foster staggered breathlessly into town to tell of his

[13] *Ibid.*, 362.

[14] Those murdered on the morning of February 23 included John Geisel and his sons, John, Henry, and Andrew; John Seroc and two children; Benjamin Wright, John Poland, Patrick McCulloch, W. R. Tullus, John Henley, Patrick Wagoner, John Idles, Henry Lawrence, Barney Castle, Gay C. Holcomb, Joseph Wilkinson, E. W. Howe, Martin Reed, George Reed, Lorenzo Warner, and Samuel Hendrick. *Herald*, Feb. 25, 1856. *Oregon Statesman*, March 18, 1856.

[15] Dodge, *Pioneer History of Coos and Curry Counties, Oregon*, 346–47.

[16] Parrish, "Anecdotes of Intercourse with the Indians," *loc. cit.*, 72–73.

harrowing escape from death. The ill-prepared settlement suddenly realized that the small army post would offer scant protection should the Indians besiege the town. With new determination the men left the bars and the card rooms to throw up a double plank wall, filling the space between with earth, on a bare knoll overlooking Battle Rock. Before their two-story blockhouse was finished, the whole town had settled in it.[17]

Naturally the Port Orford citizens wondered whether anyone had survived the holocaust to the south. On February 27, Dr. Rodney Glisan, the post surgeon, wrote: "We feel much anxiety to hear from Rogue River, as large columns of smoke are plainly to be seen rising up from the vicinity of the fort erected there by the whites of that place."[18]

Fort Miner was there, and its inhabitants were very much alive. Women, dressed in their party clothes, worked in the cabins melting lead and pouring Minié balls for the men defending the rampart. For several days the refugees had kept the Tututni at bay. Enos, proudly mounted on a white stallion, rode back and forth on the hills to the east of the fort, haranguing his warriors to storm the position. In spite of his encouragement the Indians remained mostly out of range and limited their offensive to showering the enclosure with volleys of arrows, killing livestock, and burning the rest of the settlements.

The refugees knew that their fate depended upon armed assistance, and, unaware that Foster had escaped to Fort Orford, they feared that no one knew of their plight. In hopes that a coastal steamer might pass their post, they flew an American flag and stretched a canvas banner reading "HELP" between poles on the roof of one cabin.[19]

Eight venturesome members of the Port Orford volun-

---

[17] Dodge, *Pioneer History of Coos and Curry Counties, Oregon*, 285–86. William Winsor, "Diary, 1856" (MS). Glisan, *A Journal of Army Life*, 259.
[18] *A Journal of Army Life*, 285–86.
[19] Dodge, *Pioneer History of Coos and Curry Counties, Oregon*, 307.

teers, on a foolhardy mission, rowed down the coast to see what had happened. The detachment braved the surf off Humbug Mountain but recklessly attempted to beach its whaleboat near the refugees' post. The craft overturned in the breakers, drowning six of the party. The men from the fort rescued two chilled and frightened survivors.[20]

The first week in March, with no sign of troops and less Indian activity about their post, some of the refugees decided to hike to a potato field a half-mile away on the bank of the river. The men fell ready victims to ambush, and only two of the seven foragers regained the stockade. A different mission fared much better. Charles Brown, a miner who had been on good terms with the Tututni, used his past actions as his passport to negotiate for the release of the Geisel captives. The Indians agreed to his offers of blankets and freed Christina and her daughters.[21]

Unknown to the refugees at Fort Miner, attempts were under way to rescue them from their isolated outpost. Within days of the massacre, Captain William Tichenor sailed to Crescent City to notify the government troops stationed there about the warfare on Oregon's south coast. Passing along the shore, Tichenor witnessed a terrifying spectacle. The communities which he had done so much to publicize and upon which he based the future worth of his lands at Port Orford were all destroyed. He recalled: "All along the coast was nothing but a blaze; wherever there was a log hut it was in flames or in smouldering ruins."[22]

Sending his ship on to San Francisco to carry news of the hostilities, Tichenor remained in Crescent City to guide the

[20] Reinhart, *The Golden Frontier*, 96. Dodge, *Pioneer History of Coos and Curry Counties, Oregon,* 78, Appendix, 58. Winsor, "Diary," *loc. cit.* Those who drowned were H. G. Gerow, John O' Brien, Sylvester Long, William Thompson, Richard Gay, and Felix McCue. *Oregon Statesman*, March 18, 1856.

[21] *Oregon Statesman*, March 18, 1856. Dodge, *Pioneer History of Coos and Curry Counties, Oregon,* 347–48.

[22] "Among the Oregon Indians," *loc. cit.*, 46–47.

177

army forces preparing to march to the Rogue River. Captain DeLancey Floyd-Jones, commander at the northern California port city, had been stationed there for less than two months. Although Tichenor urged him to get his men into the field at once the captain waited for orders from department headquarters.[23]

On March 6 seventy reinforcements for Crescent City and forty soldiers for Fort Orford left San Francisco. Captain E. O. C. Ord, later a famous Civil War general, delivered the instructions to Floyd-Jones. Colonel Robert C. Buchanan assumed command and immediately put the company through a hurried howitzer drill in preparation for the coming campaign. The other troops sailed to Fort Orford, where they were joined on the eleventh by seventy-four soldiers from Fort Vancouver under Captain Christopher C. Augur.[24]

General Wool hoped first to secure the mouth of the Rogue River and relieve the pioneers at Fort Miner. His two-prong operation was under way by March 15, when the Crescent City troops set out on the trail and the companies at Fort Orford made their final preparations for a similar journey. Buchanan marched his men through the virgin redwood forests between Lake Earl and Smith River. They found that the Tolowas had joined the hostile Indians. The burned cabins, newly erected grave markers, and strayed stock told the men that they might expect trouble anywhere along the trail to Gold Beach.[25]

At the Chetco River the soldiers found the ruins of the cabin built by the "exterminator" Miller. His bloody treachery had not been forgotten. The troops salvaged potatoes and cabbages from his garden. "This was a Godsend to us poor soldiers," wrote Captain Ord, "for Uncle Sam doesn't furnish

[23] *Ibid.*, 48–49. Fred B. Rogers, "Early Military Posts of Del Norte County," *California Historical Society Quarterly*, Vol. XXVI, No. 1 (1947), 1.

[24] *Alta California*, March 6, 13, 1856. Glisan, *A Journal of Army Life,* 292. Edward O. C. Ord, "The Rogue River Indian Expedition of 1856 (Diary of Capt. E. O. C. Ord)," (MS), 25.

[25] Ord, "Rogue River Indian Expedition of 1856," *loc. cit.*, 26–27.

them with anything of the sort better than rice and tough old beans."[26]

Arrogant and careless, the volunteers from Crescent City rushed ahead of the regular troops so that they might be the first to come to the relief of the people at Fort Miner. Their leader was George H. Abbot, the murderer of the Coquilles in 1854. On March 18 his force walked into an ambush in the sand dunes on the southern shore of Pistol River. Had these men traveled with the main body of troops, bloodshed might have been averted; but, being anxious to "punish" the Rogues, they stumbled into a day-long battle. The volunteers were caught in the open and only avoided a complete rout by hiding in the driftwood until the regular troops came to their rescue. They lost one man in the conflict.[27]

Three days later the government troops and the Crescent City Guard arrived at Fort Miner. Since the ferry had been destroyed, the main body of the company camped among the ruins of Gold Beach on the south shore. While the men were setting up their tents and burying the mutilated bodies of some of the victims of the massacre, the Port Orford company marched in from the north. Fort Miner was safe from imminent attack. "A queer place it was," wrote Ord, "and queer people they were in it. The Children were playing outside, glad of a chance to get out after their month's confinement. There were rough buck-skin-clad miners and mule-drivers, thick-lipped flabby squaws, delicate-looking American women ... and a general mixture of all the mongrel and nondescript races of the mines crowded together in the little fort."[28]

As the soldiers well expected, the women poured out a torrent of commentary on their harrowing experiences. Christina Geisel, her arm bandaged because of a deep stab wound received while fighting for her sons, described her captivity:

[26] *Ibid*. Sgt. Jones [Edward O. C. Ord], "Soldiering in Oregon," *Harper's Magazine*, Vol. XIII (1856), 525.

[27] Ord, "Rogue River Indian Expedition of 1856," *loc. cit.*, 27. Tichenor, "Among the Oregon Indians," *loc. cit.*, 55.

[28] Jones, "Soldiering in Oregon," *loc. cit.*, 523–24.

"Dey give us blenty to eat, and blenty of hard work to do. Dey kills ever so many cattle—sometimes two, dree in von day."[29]

The women did not have long to polish their stories, for on March 22 the schooner *Gold Beach* crossed the Rogue bar to take them and their children to a safer refuge at Port Orford. At once a quarrel developed about whether the Indian women who had spent the siege in the fort with their "husbands" were to be allowed to go also. To settle the matter, Tichenor, a recent member of the territorial legislature, offered to marry the couples in question. A half-dozen men refused the bonds of matrimony and walked away from the proceedings. Charles Brown, the man who had risked his life for the captives, and Jack Smith, however, remained faithful to their "wives" and were married at the fort that day.

Captain Ord vividly described Brown's wedding:

> The pair held a short consultation with the Colonel; and then the woman was called forward, and there on the banks of the Rogue River, by the shore of the great Pacific, with a circle of rough-looking miners standing around, the marriage ceremony was performed. Charley promised to have her, and her only, for his lawful wedded wife, and then translated the words of the ceremony for the benefit of his dusky tatooed bride. She grunted out some rough Indian gutterals in reply, and the knot was tied. There was no kissing the bride, and no wedding feast.

The chronicler concluded: "I could not help thinking that his determination to cling to the poor brown woman for better or for worse, while the prospect before them was all 'worse' and no 'better,' showed that there was some honest manhood in the rough fellow."[30] The two new wives joined the twenty other adults and fourteen children aboard the *Gold Beach*. Most of the men remained with the regular soldiers to fight the Indians.[31]

29 *Ibid.*, 524–25.
30 Ord, "Rogue River Indian Expedition of 1856," *loc. cit.*, 29. Jones, "Soldiering in Oregon," *loc. cit.*, 525.
31 Glisan, *A Journal of Army Life*, 302.

Colonel Robert Buchanan, commander of the coast operations, next hoped to carry out the second phase of General Wool's strategy. Wool had ordered his forces to converge on the Indian stronghold near the junction of the Illinois and Rogue rivers. Augur was to lead the regulars from Fort Orford; Captain Andrew J. Smith was to sweep through the forests and canyons with the troops from Fort Lane; Buchanan's men were to cut through the mountains south of the Rogue River to converge on the rendezvous site.

Timing and terrain foiled these plans. Augur's company crossed the coastal ridges through the watershed of Euchre Creek and reached the meadows at the river forks on March 19. His troops burned the villages, skirmished with the Shasta Costas, and killed five men. When the other regulars did not appear, the command journeyed to the mouth of the river, where it found Buchanan and his forces encamped. The troops from Fort Lane reached the rendezvous area about March 22, three days too late. Smith's men exchanged shots with the Rogues and suffered two casualties; then they continued over the hills to Fort Orford, where they arrived "totally without provisions and nearly naked."[32]

Buchanan hesitated to commit his forces to the wilderness when spring rains and insufficient supplies threatened to thwart his success in the field. Instead of acting precipitously, he dispatched Captains Ord and Floyd-Jones with 112 men for a foray up the river to the principal Mikonotunne village located on a meadow near Skookum House Prairie. The soldiers reached their goal without mishap, but, when they began to burn the plank houses and stores abandoned by the fleeing Indians, the Rogues commenced a sharp barrage. At least five warriors died in the close combat in the village, and another three drowned when the last defenders tried to flee in their canoes.

Ord feared to take up the chase, for he knew that the

[32] *Ibid.*, 296–98, 308. "Post Returns of Fort Orford, Oregon, 1849–1856" (MS).

181

Indians had the advantage in their old haunts. The soldiers decided to withdraw at once and began their return march. They rigged makeshift litters to carry two privates who were wounded in the battle and retraced their route until darkness overtook them in the forest. They arrived the next morning at Buchanan's base camp near Fort Miner. Their mission had been the first to dislodge the Rogues from one of their strong-holds during the months-old war.[33]

While these troops were in the field, some of the Coquilles whom Wright had brought to a temporary reservation at Port Orford in December decided to go home. A company of vol-unteers overtook them, killed twenty, and captured forty women and children. They returned the prisoners to the army garrison at Port Orford.[34]

Troop movement commenced again in March in the interior of the Rogue country; mounting Indian hostility spurred the volunteers to action. On March 23 the Rogues ambushed a pack train on the trail between Crescent City and the Illinois Valley, killing four men and capturing twenty-eight mules loaded with supplies and ammunition. Late in the month they skirmished with volunteers patrolling Cow Creek in the Umpqua Mountains.[35]

These troubles and the arrival of spring spurred the main volunteer forces to get into the field. On April 16, James Bruce put his battalion on the trail, and the next day William Lat-shaw ordered his men out of winter quarters. The soldiers took rations for twenty-five days, picks, shovels, and canvas boats to help them on their campaign to dislodge the Rogues in the canyon in the coast mountains.[36]

By April 23 the joint command of 535 men was encamped at Little Meadows. They found a large number of Indians

[33] Ord, "Rogue River Indian Expedition of 1856," *loc. cit.*, 31–32. Jones, "Soldiering in Oregon," *loc. cit.*, 525–26. "Post Returns of Fort Orford, Oregon, 1848–1856," *loc. cit.*
[34] *Oregon Statesman*, April 15, 1856.
[35] *Ibid.*, April 18, 1856. *Table Rock Sentinel*, April 19, 1856.
[36] *Oregon Statesman*, April 22, 1856.

between there and the Big Meadows, closer to the Big Bend than they had been the previous November. Days passed as Bruce and Latshaw deployed detachments to try to draw the enemy into a position where they could be attacked, but there was little success. Finally on April 27 the commanders decided to march through the mountains and descend the precipitous bluffs to fire across the river into the Indian camp. One hundred soldiers crossed the ridges, concealed by a heavy fog, and positioned themselves in the brush on the riverbank.

On order they launched their surprise attack. The Indian women grabbed their children and ran for the forest while the men attempted to return the murderous fire. Reinforcements, which doubled the attacking forces during the afternoon, enabled the volunteers to keep up their assault until dusk. They lost but one man while twenty or thirty Indians died in the struggle. Although the Rogues cried for peace throughout the day, the troops were in no mood to stop the war.[37]

At last the volunteers had met the enemy and won a victory. They withdrew to Big Meadows and renewed the battle the next day when they found some Indians along the river. The skirmish was minor, for neither of the opposing forces dared to cross and risk a direct assault.[38]

By the first of May the volunteers had nearly exhausted their supplies. The snow was still deep on the mountain trails, hindering pack trains communicating with the depot at Grave Creek. There was no sign of the government troops pushing up the river, and since many of the wounded men required medical attention, several of the companies left the Big Meadows. These forces traveled over the old Indian trail to Camas Valley before hitting the Umpqua Valley route to their headquarters at Camp Leland. Five companies remained in the mountains to build a stockade, which they dubbed Fort

[37] *Ibid.*, May 20, 1856. *Table Rock Sentinel*, May 17, 1856.
[38] *Oregon Statesman*, May 20, 1856.

Lamerick in honor of John Lamerick, one of their leaders from Jacksonville.[39]

After the expedition to the Mikonotunne village, the regular troops at the mouth of the Rogue and at Fort Orford settled down for several weeks of inaction. To be sure, small parties searched for trails up the river toward the junction of the Illinois and the Rogue, but most of the men were playing cards, reading, and "mineralizing." That is, they were prospecting and trying to make the most of a miserable camp in the wind, rain, and hail of March and April on the southwestern Oregon coast.[40]

The survivors of the Gold Beach Guard, supplemented by new recruits, were as anxious as ever to find the enemy. On April 22 the company went up the Rogue as far as the mouth of Lobster Creek. The men quietly concealed themselves on the massive boulders fronting the river at that point and waited. Shortly after sunrise two canoes containing twelve men and three women came down the stream. When they passed under the rocks, the volunteers opened fire and killed all but three of the unsuspecting people.[41]

Near the end of the month the companies of regulars prepared for action. To obtain adequate provisions for an extended campaign in the mountains, Buchanan had purchased several loads of supplies in Crescent City. He ordered E. O. C. Ord and a detachment of troops to escort the packers on their return journey from headquarters on the Rogue to the California boundary. When the mules and men were fording the Chetco River, the Indians attacked. Ord pursued seventy of the foe up the stream, but they hid in the alder and willow along the banks and continued firing on the men caught in the middle of the river. The troops killed several of the enemy, but lost one sergeant, who was mortally wounded in hand-to-hand combat with an Indian he had driven into the water.[42]

[39] *Ibid.*
[40] Ord, "Rogue River Indian Expedition of 1856," *loc. cit.*, 40.
[41] Winsor, "Diary," *loc. cit. Oregon Statesman*, May 20, 1856.
[42] Ord, "Rogue River Indian Expedition of 1856," *loc. cit.*, 41–45.

Buchanan finally launched the campaign up the river on the eighth of May. He split his forces, sending companies under Smith and Augur along the north bank, while taking those of Ord, Reynolds, and Floyd-Jones under his personal command up the south side. The colonel should have heeded the advice of his scouts, for his soldiers were soon forced miles off their objective by the rugged terrain. The rough going was bad enough, but Buchanan's moods and ill humor were all the more discouraging for his troops. Ord, who received much of his commanding officer's spleen, wrote: "Think old fellow if he get through this campaign all right will be disposed to put on *airs* is little so *now*—and disposed to be unamiable has made enemies of most all the officers already."[43]

Buchanan's men, after an arduous journey through country still covered with snow, reached the meadows at Oak Flats on the Illinois on the fifteenth. Here the colonel conferred with several Indian leaders whose people were hiding in the area. Smith, whose companies had arrived at the mouth of the Illinois some days previously, brought more Indians to the conference grounds. The preliminary discussions were concluded when the bands from the Chetco, Pistol River, Euchre Creek, and the mouth of the Rogue River promised to surrender. "Limpy" and "George," two of the war leaders who had survived the exodus from the valley, met Buchanan on the nineteenth. They were more than ready to stop fighting but did not want to leave their homeland for the coast reservation as the army leader demanded. However, the two leaders finally capitulated and agreed to assemble their people in seven days at the "Meadows" at the Big Bend of the Rogue.[44]

Acting in accord with these plans, Captain Smith and a detachment of infantrymen marched up the river to meet the surrendering Indians at the Big Bend. Drenching rains soaked the soldiers and delayed the arrival of the people com-

[43] *Ibid.*, 47–49.
[44] "Consolidated File of Reports Relating to the Expedition Against the Rogue River Indians in the Spring of 1856" (MS).

ing down the river by canoe or over the muddy trails. On the twenty-sixth the Indians told Smith that "George" was but nine miles away; he was bringing with him survivors of the Applegate, Galice Creek, and Cow Creek bands.

The soldiers were confident that the rendezvous would end the war, for the Rogues truly desired peace. The months of flight, hunger, and uncertainty had reduced them to desperation, and they knew that the volunteers pushing them from up river would make no magnanimous offer of amnesty should they be willing to go to a reservation. Before they arrived at the Big Bend, however, the volunteers struck.

When reinforcements arrived at Fort Lamerick on May 24, the companies quartered there resumed their offensive. While the wounded, defeated Indians struggled through the canyon to the government troops, the volunteers cut them down. They raked the rapids with deadly fire as canoeloads of people tried to escape to the Big Bend. Other volunteers shot at the Indians hurrying along the trails on the opposite bank of the river.[45]

Captain Smith sensed that something was wrong. The Indians, who had at first seemed so eager for peace, grew sullen and afraid. Their fears became hostility as more and more of their people arrived, bringing tales of the massacres under way a few miles up the river, and they suspected, rightly, that the soldiers, regular and volunteer, were gathering them at the Big Bend for the final execution of their race.

The Indians became so menacing that Smith prudently decided to station his forces on the ridge behind the open meadows. On the morning of the twenty-seventh, as more Rogues poured into the rendezvous site, Smith readied his men for trouble, but warned them not to fire the first shot. About eleven that morning the Rogues charged the ridge. Only the steady fire of the howitzer and a forward assault of the troops enabled the soldiers to stem the advance. The Indians, well knowing that this might be the last battle of their

[45] *Oregon Statesman*, June 24, 1856.

lives, climbed the hills surrounding the position and maintained a vicious crossfire on Smith's company throughout the day. The soldiers suffered so many casualties that they had to withdraw one flank of their troops. By dusk fifteen men lay wounded and four were dead.[46]

The Rogues kept up their offensive throughout the evening, but shortly before midnight Lieutenant Nelson B. Sweitzer was able to construct a breastwork of packs, blankets, saddles, and trenches on the far end of the ridge, just where it crumbled and plunged two hundred feet into Foster Creek. Most of the wounded men hid in these defenses; other soldiers stationed themselves in rifle pits along the crest of the hill.

The attack resumed anew about four in the morning. For the next twelve hours the Indians made several sallies toward the soldiers' line, but were driven back each time. Late in the afternoon, some thirty hours after the battle began, the thirsty, exhausted men at the Big Bend heard the shouts and the muskets of Captain C. C. Augur's troops. Charles Foster, one of Smith's guides, had escaped from the Big Bend and reported the precarious situation to the soldiers waiting down the river. The fresh forces drove the Indians to the riverbank, where many of them surrendered. The number of warriors killed was not reported, but Smith and Augur had seven men killed and twenty wounded.[47]

On the last day of the month the volunteers from Fort Lamerick arrived at the Big Bend. This "hard looking set" came to the regulars' camp and "talked big and made threats," as Captain Ord noted in his diary. While the men waited for the Indians to assemble and Superintendent Palmer conferred with the headmen, detachments of soldiers went downstream to try to drive the hostile bands out of the hills near Copper Canyon. On June 5, John Reynolds' company burned a village

[46] "Consolidated File of Reports Relating to the Expedition Against the Rogue River Indians in the Spring of 1856," *loc. cit.*
[47] *Ibid.*

187

occupied by Shasta Costas and killed four men who were fishing at a large weir in the river.[48]

Augur's men and the Gold Beach Guard dropped down to Painted Rock to scout for refugees. The volunteers killed eight men, captured a dozen women and children, and seized four canoes. The regulars killed six persons and reported that many Indians drowned when their canoes overturned in the rapids.[49]

For several days Indian stragglers continued to gather at the Big Bend. In spite of the rigors of war, the Rogues played shinny and tossed gambling sticks to pass the time. Ord described some of their activities:

> The Ind[ian]s gathered in a circle crowd of soldiers around— and their mimic wardance—began some dozen or more shoulder to shoulder singing and beating time with their feet—tis a pretty moonlight night and the secluded mountain gourges ring with the reverbarated whoops from the dancers—at the same time and but a few yards off from the crowd of brush huts and low blanket tents issues the never-ending melancholy wail of the squaws in mourning.[50]

During the hot June days the blind, lame, sick, fearful people yet gathered. On the tenth the cavalcade of soldiers and prisoners set out for Port Orford. Ord was deeply stirred about forcing these people to leave on a long journey to an unknown land. "It almost makes me shed tears to listen to them wailing as they totter along," he wrote, as the final exodus began through the mountains.[51]

While the people were on the trail, the volunteers from the Rogue Valley and the coast searched for refugees and fought skirmishes at Pistol River and the Chetco. They brought the Indians they captured to the garrison at Port Orford. On June 20 the steamer *Columbia* left the small

[48] Ord, "Rogue River Indian Expedition of 1856," *loc. cit.*, 54–57.
[49] Winsor, "Diary," *loc. cit. Oregon Statesman*, July 1, 1856.
[50] Ord, "Rogue River Indian Expedition of 1856," *loc. cit.*, 58–59.
[51] *Ibid.*

harbor with 600 persons aboard. These Indians sailed up the coast to Astoria, up the Columbia River to Fort Vancouver, up the Willamette River to the Yamhill; then they boarded barges for a short passage toward the coast mountains. At the head of navigation they began a forced march through the hills to their new home on the Siletz Reservation.[52]

"John," the last hostile leader in southern Oregon, surrendered near Port Orford at the end of June. The wily old man had kept together 35 men, 90 women, and 90 children of his band. Since the *Columbia* was taking a full load of 592 additional persons to the reservation, "John's" band was compelled to walk nearly 125 miles up the coast.[53]

Although the Indians suffered on their long journey, either by land or by sea, they were fortunate compared to the stragglers left scattered through the hills of southern Oregon. During the summer and the following winter, the refugees were hunted down, murdered, and, occasionally, captured. The government hired William Tichenor to bring those survivors he could find to the new reservation. After eight months in the field, he had found 152 holdouts. The "fire-eaters" ambushed these half-naked, starving Indians when they were camped near the charred ruins of the cabin of John Geisel. When the captives marched on, they left the bodies of 19 of their kinsmen in the forest.[54]

The rains came again to the Rogue country. The streams cleared as the miners rushed away for new diggings and pursued richer dreams of wealth. Along the mountain creeks the beaver gnawed the maple, the alder, and the dogwood. Sea otter yet swam and dived in the surf near the coast. In the summers the smelt returned to the coarse sand beaches, and in the fall the salmon surged up the streams, fought against the riffles and the rapids, and returned to their spawning grounds. Acorns formed, dried, and fell from the oaks. Camas lilies

[52] *Ibid.*, 59. Glisan, *A Journal of Army Life*, 346–47.
[53] Glisan, *A Journal of Army Life*, 348–50.
[54] Tichenor, "Among the Oregon Indians," *loc. cit.*, 28–31, 102.

bloomed white and blue in the meadows—yet all was different in this land.

No longer did the buckskin-clad women, wearing their basket caps, wander through the fields with their digging sticks and collecting baskets. No longer did the stakes and poles of the weirs channel the salmon into netting ponds in the rivers. Sand and grass crept into the house pits amid the charred and rotting planks scattered along the river bars. Moss and lichens inched across the boulders to fill the rock mortars where for centuries the pestles had ground the acorns into flour for leaching. Occasionally the sun reflected from the iridescent fragments of shattered mussel and abalone shell, but never again would new layers of pearly refuse be tossed on the middens.

The opening of southwestern Oregon had begun slowly— ships of discovery sailing along the coast, a hearty band of fur trappers, a botanist seeking cones and twigs, the government exploring expeditions, and the surveying of the Southern Emigrant Route. Then the influx accelerated with the boom of gold rush and the scramble for donation land claims. The wealth of the Rogue country—furs, gold, rich lands, timber—was responsible for luring the white man.

The opening of this region was little different from the conquest of other frontiers in western America. The long-familiar elements of the frontier experience—the trapper, the trader, the cattle drover, the miner, and the settler—were all present. Nor was the resistance of the Indians unique; their desire to retain their homeland was only natural. Nevertheless, the forces of the newcomers, their diseases, vices, tools, and technology spelled change for the Rogues.

Change in the Rogue country was tragedy for her first people. The nearly ninety-five hundred Indians who had held this land when the white men first penetrated it became in increasing numbers victims of "civilization." The wars, the massacres, and the final struggles of 1855–56 forced the bands through the mountains in their exodus to the sea. Then over the Pacific, on the smoky, rumbling old steamer *Columbia*, the two thousand survivors journeyed north to the reservation, a land that had never held the bones of their ancestors or heard their chants, their shouts at the shinny game, or the singing of the shamans.

Near the spruce thickets north of the mouth of the Rogue River, near a clearing in the forest where once stood the cabin of a German settler and his family, near the weathering granite marker inscribed with the fate of those pioneers named Geisel, still lay the scattered and unburied bones of the last of the Rogues on their way from their homeland.

BIBLIOGRAPHY

I. Unpublished Manuscripts

Miscellaneous

B 223/a/5, MS, Hudson's Bay Company Archives, London, England.

B 223/b/15, fo. 33, MS, Hudson's Bay Company Archives, London, England.

B 223/b/39, fo. 95d, MS, Hudson's Bay Company Archives, London, England.

Cardwell, James A. "Emigrant Company." MS P–A 15, Bancroft Library, Berkeley, Calif.

Davidson, T. L. "By the Southern Route into Oregon." MS P–A 23, Bancroft Library, Berkeley, Calif.

Deady, Matthew Paul. "Letters, Dictations, and Related Biographical Material, 1874–1889." MS P–A 161, Bancroft Library, Berkeley, Calif.

Dowell, B. F. MS P–A 133, Bancroft Library, Berkeley, Calif.

———. "Scrapbook, 1855–63." MS P–A 134, Bancroft Library, Berkeley, Calif.

———. "Newspaper Cuttings." MS P–A 136, Bancroft Library, Berkeley, Calif.

———. "Oregon Indian War, Principally the War of 1855–56 in Southern Oregon." MSS P–A 137, P–A 138, Bancroft Library, Berkeley, Calif.

———. "Dowell's Biographies." MS P–A 139, Bancroft Library, Berkeley, Calif.

Duncan, L. J. C. "Settlement in Southern Oregon." MS P–A 27, Bancroft Library, Berkeley, Calif.

Eld, Henry. "Sketchbook No. 2." MS, Yale University Library, New Haven, Conn.

———. "Sketchbook No. 3." MS, Yale University Library, New Haven, Conn.

Gibbs, Addison C. "Notes on the History of Oregon." MS P–A 36, Bancroft Library, Berkeley, Calif.

Giles, Daniel. "Autobiography of Daniel Giles." MS, Mrs. Claude Giles, Coos Bay, Ore.

Harry, John Alva. "Diary, 1854–56." MS, Mr. Joe Harry, Coos Bay, Ore.

Lane, Joseph. "Autobiography." MS P–A 43, Bancroft Library, Berkeley, Calif.

Menzies, Archibald. "A. Menzies Journal of Vancouver's Voyage, 1790–1794." MS Add 32,641, British Museum, London, England.

Minto, John. "Early Days of Oregon." MS P–A 50, Bancroft Library, Berkeley, Calif.

"Minutes of Council, Northern Department, 1832/50." MS, Hudson's Bay Company Archives, London, England.

"Notes on Coos Bay." MS P–A 86–87, Bancroft Library, Berkeley, Calif.

Ord, Edward O. C. "The Rogue River Indian Expedition of 1856 (Diary of Capt. E.O.C. Ord)," ed. by Ellen Frances Ord. Unpublished Master's Thesis, Bancroft Library, Berkeley, Calif.

Parrish, Josiah L. "Anecdotes of Intercourse with the Indians." MS P–A 59, Bancroft Library, Berkeley, Calif.

Puget, Peter. "Log of Discovery, 1791–1792." MS Ad. 55, #27, Public Record Office, London, England.

Ream, Daniel. "Autobiographical Dictation." MS C–D 954, Bancroft Library, Berkeley, Calif.

Ross, John E. "Narrative of an Indian Fighter." MS P–A 63, Bancroft Library, Berkeley, Calif.

Smith, Jedediah, William Sublette, and David E. Jackson. "A Brief Sketch of accidents, misfortunes, and depredations committed by Indians, etc., on the firm of Smith, Jackson, and Sublette, since July 1826 to the present 24th, 1829." MS, Clark Collection, Kansas State Historical Society, Topeka, Kansas.

Tichenor, William. "Among the Oregon Indians." MS P–A 84, Bancroft Library, Berkeley, Calif.

"Tututni." BAE MS 72, Office of Anthropology, Smithsonian Institution, Washington, D.C.

Williams, L[orin] L. "First Settlements in Southwestern Oregon. T'Vault's Expedition." MS P–A 77, Bancroft Library, Berkeley, Calif.

Winsor, William. "Diary, 1856." MS, Mr. Richard Fisk, Gold Beach, Ore.

National Archives, Washington, D.C.

RG 77: Records of the Office of the Chief of Engineers—

Alvord, B[enjamin]. MS, "Sketch of the Military Road 'From Myrtle Creek Umpqua Valley to Camp Stuart Rogue River Valley,' Oregon Territory, Located in the Autumn of the year 1853."

Cram, Tho[mas] Jefferson. MS, "Military Topographical Memoir and Report on the Department of the Pacific."

Williamson, R[obert] S[tockton]. MS, "Sketch of the Umpqua and Rogue Rivers, & Intermediate Country, from a Reconnaissance by R. S. Williamson, Lieut. U. S. Topl. Engrs. while attached to the Command of Maj. P. Kearny, 1st Dragoons, and Lieut. Col. S. Casey, 2nd Infy. 1851."

RG 94: Records of the Adjutant General's Office—
MS, "Post Returns of Fort Orford, Oregon, 1849–1856."

RG 98: Records of U.S. Army Commands—
MS, "Consolidated File of Reports Relating to the Expedition against the Rogue River Indians in the Spring of 1856."

RG 99: Records of the Office of the Paymaster General—
Mansfield, Joseph K. F. MS, "Col. Mansfield's Inspection Report of the Dept. of Pacific, 1855." Misc. File #282.

II. GOVERNMENT PUBLICATIONS

Annual Report of the Commissioner of Indian Affairs, 1854. Washington, D.C., Government Printing Office, 1855.

Davidson, George. *Pacific Coast: Coast Pilot of California, Oregon, and Washington Territory.* Washington, D.C., Government Printing Office, 1869.

Heitman, Francis B. *Historical Register and Dictionary of the United States Army, From Its Organization, September 29, 1789, to March 2, 1903.* 2 vols. Washington, D.C., Government Printing Office, 1903.

Hodge, Frederick Webb (ed.). *Handbook of American Indians North of Mexico.* 2 vols. (Smithsonian Institution, Bureau of American Ethnology *Bulletin 30.*) Washington, D.C., Government Printing Office, 1910.

Journal of the Proceedings of the Council of the Legislative Assembly of Oregon Territory, Ninth Regular Session—1857–8. Salem, Ore., 1857.

Kappler, Charles J. (ed.). *Indian Affairs: Laws and Treaties. II. Treaties.* Washington, D.C., Government Printing Office, 1904.

United States Congress, House. *House Exec. Doc. No. 2, 32* Cong., 1 sess.

———. *House Exec. Doc. No. 1, 32* Cong., 2 sess.

———. *House Exec. Doc. No. 1, 33* Cong., 1 sess.

———. *House Exec. Doc. No. 99, 33* Cong., 1 sess.

———. *House Exec. Doc. No. 93, 34* Cong., 1 sess.

———. *House Exec. Doc. No. 76, 34* Cong., 3 sess.

———, *House Exec. Doc. No. 52, 38* Cong., 2 sess.

———. *House Misc. Doc. No. 47, 35* Cong., 2 sess.

United States Congress, Senate. *Senate Exec. Doc. No. 4, 33* Cong., special sess.

———. *Senate Exec. Doc. No. 16, 33* Cong., 2 sess.

———. *Senate Misc. Doc. No. 59, 36* Cong., 1 sess.

III. NEWSPAPERS

Alta California (San Francisco, Calif.).

Ashland Tidings (Ashland, Ore.).

California Farmer (San Francisco, Calif.).

Herald (Crescent City, Calif.).

Oregon Sentinel (Jacksonville, Ore.).

Oregon Spectator (Oregon City, Ore.).

Oregon Statesman (Oregon City, Corvallis, Salem, Ore.).

Plaindealer (Roseburg, Ore.).

Table Rock Sentinel (Jacksonville, Ore.).

IV. BOOKS

Bancroft, Hubert Howe. *History of Oregon, 1834–1848.* San Francisco, The History Company, 1886.

————. *History of Oregon, 1848–1888.* San Francisco, The History Company, 1888.

Beeson, John. *A Plea for the Indians: With Facts and Features of the Late War in Oregon.* New York, John Beeson, 1858.

Clark, Ella E. *Indian Legends of the Pacific Northwest.* Berkeley, University of California Press, 1953.

Clarke, S. A. *Pioneer Days of Oregon History.* 2 vols. Portland, Ore., J. K. Gill Co., 1905.

Clyman, James. *James Clyman, Frontiersman: The Adventures of a Trapper and Covered-Wagon Emigrant as Told in His Own Reminiscences and Diaries.* Ed. by Charles L. Camp. Portland, Ore., Champoeg Press, 1960.

Colvocoresses, George M. *Four Years in a Government Exploring Expedition.* New York, Cornish, Lamport & Co., 1852.

Corney, Peter. *Voyages in the Northern Pacific.* Honolulu, Thos. G. Thrum, 1896.

Crook, George. *General George Crook: His Autobiography.* Ed. by Martin Schmitt. Norman, University of Oklahoma Press, 1960.

Curtis, Edward S. *The Hupa, Yurok, Karok, Wiyot, Tolowa and Tututni, Shasta, Klamath.* (*The North American Indian: Being a Series of Volumes Picturing and Describing the Indians of the U.S. and Alaska.* Ed. by Frederick Webb Hodge. Vol. XIII.) Cambridge, Mass., University Press, 1924.

Dodge, Orvil. *Pioneer History of Coos and Curry Counties, Oregon.* Salem, Ore., Capital Printing Co., 1898.

DuBois, Cora. "The Wealth Concept as an Integrating Factor in Tolowa-Tututni Culture," in *Essays in Anthropology Presented to A. L. Kroeber.* Berkeley, Calif., 1936.

Edwards, Philip L. *The Diary of Philip Leget Edwards: The Great Cattle Drive from California to Oregon in 1857.* San Francisco, Grabhorn Press, 1932.

Gibson, Horatio G. *Efforts of Speech and Pen.* [San Francisco, n.p., n.d.]

Gibbs, George. "Journal of the Expedition of Colonel Redick M'Kee, United States Indian Agent, through North-western California. Performed in the Summer and Fall of 1851," in *Information Respecting the History, Condition, and Prospects of the Indian Tribes of the United States,* ed. by H. R. School-

197

craft. Pt. III, 99–177. Philadelphia, Lippincott, Grambo & Co., 1853.

Glisan, Rodney. *A Journal of Army Life.* San Francisco, A. L. Bancroft Co., 1874.

Hafen, LeRoy R. (ed.). *The Mountain Men and the Fur Trade of the Far West.* Vol. I. Glendale, Calif., Arthur H. Clark Co., 1965.

Hastings, Lansford W. *The Emigrant's Guide to Oregon and California.* Princeton, Princeton University Press, 1932.

Hines, Gustavus. *Wild Life in Oregon.* New York, Hurst & Co., 1881.

Holmes, Kenneth L. *Ewing Young: Master Trapper.* Portland, Ore., Binfords & Mort, Publishers, 1967.

Howay, Frederick W. (ed.). *Voyages of the* Columbia *to the Northwest Coast, 1787–1790 and 1790–1793.* (Massachusetts Historical Society *Collections,* Vol. LXXIX.) Boston, The Massachusetts Historical Society, 1941.

Kelley, Hall J. *Hall Jackson Kelley on Oregon: A Collection of Five of His Published Works and a Number of Hitherto Unpublished Letters.* Ed. by Wilbur Powell. Princeton, Princeton University Press, 1932.

Kirkpatrick, J. M. *The Heroes of Battle Rock, Or the Miners' Reward. A Short Story of Thrilling Interest. How A Small Cannon Done Its Work. Port Orford, Oregon, the Scene of the Great Tragedy. A Desperate Encounter of Nine White Men with Three Hundred Indians. Miraculous Escape After Untold Hardships. Historically True. Savages Subdued and Rich Gold Mines Discovered.* Ed. by Orvil Dodge. [Myrtle Point, Ore.], 1904.

Meacham, Walter. *Applegate Trail.* Portland, Ore., James, Kerns & Abbott, 1947.

Minter, Harold A. *Umpqua Valley, Oregon, and Its Pioneers.* Portland, Ore., Binfords & Mort, Publishers, 1967.

Murray, Keith A. *The Modocs and Their War.* Norman, University of Oklahoma Press, 1959.

Peterson, Emil R., and Alfred Powers. *A Century of Coos and Curry.* Portland, Ore., Binfords and Mort, 1952.

Pfeiffer, Ida. *A Lady's Second Journey Round the World.* New York, Harper & Bros., 1856.

Poesch, Jessie. *Titian Ramsay Peale, 1799–1885, and His Journals of the Wilkes Expedition.* (Memoirs of the American Philosophical Society, Volume 52.) Philadelphia, The American Philosophical Society, 1961.

Reinhart, Herman Francis. *The Golden Frontier: The Recollections of Herman Francis Reinhart, 1851–1869.* Ed. by Doyce B. Nunis, Jr. Austin, University of Texas Press, 1962.

Rich, E. E. (ed.). *The Letters of John McLoughlin from Fort Vancouver to the Governor and Committee. First Series, 1825–38.* (The Publications of the Champlain Society, Hudson's Bay Company Series, Vol. IV.) Toronto, The Champlain Society, 1941.

————. *The Letters of John McLoughlin from Fort Vancouver to the Governor and Committee. Second Series, 1839–1844.* (The Publications of the Champlain Society, Hudson's Bay Company Series, Vol. VI.) Toronto, The Champlain Society, 1943.

Riddle, George W. *Early Days in Oregon: A History of the Riddle Valley.* Myrtle Creek, Ore., Myrtle Creek Mail, 1953.

Sengstacken, Agnes Ruth. *Destination West!* Portland, Ore., Binfords & Mort, Publishers, 1942.

Settle, Raymond W. (ed.). *The March of the Mounted Riflemen.* Glendale, Calif., Arthur H. Clark Co., 1940.

Sullivan, Maurice (ed.). *The Travels of Jedediah Smith.* Santa Ana, Calif., Fine Arts Press, 1934.

Townsend, John K. *Narrative of a Journey across the Rocky Mountains, to the Columbia River.* Ed. by Reuben Gold Thwaites. (*Early Western Travels, 1748–1846,* Vol. XXI.) Cleveland, Ohio, Arthur H. Clark Co., 1905.

Victor, Frances Fuller. *The Early Indian Wars of Oregon: Compiled from the Oregon Archives and Other Original Sources with Muster Rolls.* Salem, Ore., F. C. Baker, 1894.

Walker, Joel P. *A Pioneer of Pioneers: Narrative of Adventures thro' Alabama, Florida, New Mexico, Oregon & California, etc.* Los Angeles, G. Dawson, 1953.

Walling, A. G. *History of Southern Oregon, Comprising Jackson, Josephine, Douglas, Curry, and Coos Counties: Compiled from the Most Authentic Sources.* Portland, Ore., A. G. Walling, 1884.

V. Articles

Applegate, Lindsay. "Notes and Reminiscences of Laying out and

Establishing the Old Emigrant Road into Southern Oregon in the Year 1846," *Oregon Historical Quarterly*, Vol. XXII, No. 1 (1921), 12–45.

Barnett, H. G. "Culture Element Distributions. VII. Oregon Coast," *University of California Anthropological Records*, Vol. I, No. 3 (1937), 155–204.

Berreman, Joel V. "Tribal Distribution in Oregon," *Memoirs, American Anthropological Association*, No. 47 (1937), 7–65.

Butler, America R. "Mrs. Butler's 1853 Diary of Rogue River Valley," ed. by Oscar O. Winther and Rose Dodge Galey, *Oregon Historical Quarterly*, Vol. XLI, No. 4 (1940), 337–66.

Colvig, William M. "Indian Wars of Southern Oregon," *Oregon Historical Quarterly*, Vol. IV, No. 3 (1903), 227–40.

Cressman, Luther S. "Aboriginal Burials in Southwestern Oregon," *American Anthropologist*, Vol. XXXV (1933), 116–30.

Dement, Russell C., and Ellis S. Dement. "After the Covered Wagons," *Oregon Historical Quarterly*, Vol. LXIII, No. 1 (1962), 5–40.

Dorsey, J. Owen. "The Gentile System of the Siletz Tribes," *Journal of American Folklore*, Vol. III (1890), 227–337.

Douglas, David. "Sketch of a Journey to the Northwestern Parts of the Continent of North America, During the Years 1824–'25–'26–'27," *Oregon Historical Quarterly*, Vol. V, No. 3 (1904), 230–71; No. 4, 325–69; Vol. VI, No. 1 (1905), 76–97; No. 2, 206–27; No. 3, 288–309; No. 4, 417–49.

Drucker, Philip. "The Tolowa and Their Southwest Oregon Kin," *University of California Publications in American Archaeology and Ethnology*, Vol. XXXVI (1936), 221–300.

Elliott, T. C. "British Values in Oregon, 1847," *Oregon Historical Quarterly*, Vol. XXXII, No. 1 (1931), 27–45.

———. "The Peter Skene Ogden Journals," *Oregon Historical Quarterly*, Vol. XI, No. 2 (1910), 201–22.

Frachtenberg, Leo J. "Shasta and Athapascan Myths from Oregon," *Journal of American Folklore*, Vol. XXVIII (1915), 207–42.

Holt, Catherine. "Shasta Ethnography," *University of California Anthropological Records*, Vol. III, No. 4 (1946), 298–349.

H[opkins], C. T. "An Exploring Expedition in 1850," *Overland Monthly* (2d Series), Vol. XVII, No. 101 (1891), 475–82. [C. T. W. is given as the author of the article; however, the same text appeared as "Explorations in Oregon," *The Pioneer*, Vol. I, No. 5 (1854), 282–86; Vol. II, No. 1 (1854), 86–90, by C. T. H. Bancroft Library cites the author as C. T. H(opkins).]

Jones, Sgt. [Edward O. C. Ord]. "Soldiering in Oregon," *Harper's Magazine*, Vol. XIII (1856), 522–26.

Kroeber, Alfred L. "Basket Designs of the Indians of North-western California," *University of California Publications in American Archaeology and Ethnology*, Vol. II, No. 4 (1904), 104–64.

———. "Cultural and Natural Areas of Native North America," *University of California Publications in American Archaeology and Ethnology*, Vol. XXXVIII (1939), 1–228.

———. "Fishing among the Indians of North-Western California," *University of California Anthropological Records*, Vol. XXI (1960).

———. "Types of Indian Culture in California," *University of California Publications in American Archaeology and Ethnology*, Vol. II, No. 3 (1904), 81–103.

Lewis, A. B. "Tribes of the Columbia Valley and the Coast of Washington and Oregon," *Memoirs, American Anthropological Association*, Vol. I, Pt. 2 (1906), 147–209.

Maloney, Alice Bay. "Camp Sites of Jedediah Smith on the Oregon Coast," *Oregon Historical Quarterly*, Vol. XLI, No. 3 (1940), 304–23.

———, (ed.). "Fur Brigade to the Bonaventura: John Work's California Expedition of 1832–33 for the Hudson's Bay Company," *California Historical Society Quarterly*, Vol. XXII, No. 3 (1943), 193–222; No. 4, 323–48; Vol. XXIII, No. 1 (1944), 19–40; No. 2, 123–46.

———. "John Work of the Hudson's Bay Company: Leader of the California Brigade of 1832–33," *California Historical Society Quarterly*, Vol. XXII, No. 2 (1943), 97–109.

Rogers, Fred B. "Early Military Posts of Del Norte County," *California Historical Society Quarterly*, Vol. XXVI, No. 1 (1947), 1–11.

Santee, J. F. (ed.). "Letters of John R. Tice," *Oregon Historical Quarterly*, Vol. XXXVII (1936), 24–44.

Sapir, Edward. "Notes on the Takelma Indians of South-western Oregon," *American Anthropologist*, New Series, Vol. IX, No. 2 (1907), 251–75.

———. "Religious Ideas of the Takelma Indians of Southwestern Oregon," *Journal of American Folklore*, Vol. XX, No. 76 (1907), 33–49.

Schofield, Socrates. "The Klamath Exploring Expedition, 1850," *Oregon Historical Quarterly*, Vol. XVII, No. 4 (1916), 343–57.

Schumacher, Paul. "Researches in the Kjökkenmöddings and Graves of a Former Population of the Coasts of Oregon," *United States Geological and Geographical Survey of the Territories, Bulletin III*, No. 1 (1877), 27–35.

INDEX

203

205

208

213

The paper on which this book is printed bears the watermark of the University of Oklahoma Press and has an effective life of at least three hundred years.